EXPERIENCE HALIFAX

Where Nova Scotia's Heart Meets the Sea

BRIAN ARMSTRONG

BRIAN ARMSTRONG

Experience Halifax
Where Nova Scotia's Heart Meets the Sea

Copyright © 2025 by Brian Armstrong

All rights reserved. No part of this publication may be reproduced, stored or transmitted in any form or by any means, electronic, mechanical, photocopying, recording, scanning, or otherwise without written permission from the publisher. It is illegal to copy this book, post it to a website, or distribute it by any other means without permission.

First edition

This book was professionally typeset on Reedsy.
Find out more at reedsy.com

To the people of Halifax - past, present, and future - whose spirit of kindness, resilience, and pride makes this city shine brighter with every tide. May this book inspire locals and visitors alike to see our home through eyes of wonder.

"A great city is that which has the greatest men and women."
— Walt Whitman

"Home is more than where you're from, it's where your heart keeps returning."
— Brian Armstrong

Contents

Preface	ii
Acknowledgments	iii
Welcome to Halifax	iv
The Historic Waterfront	1
Downtown Discoveries	9
Dartmouth: Across the Harbor	16
Point Pleasant Park and the South End	24
Museums, Art and Science for All Ages	30
Parks, Trails, and the Great Outdoors	37
Coastal Drives and Day Trips	45
Food, Flavor, and Family Dining	53
Arts, Culture, and Local Spirit	62
History in Every Corner	71
Beyond Halifax: Regional Family Excursions	80
Conclusion – Halifax, the Heart of the East Coast	90
Also by Brian Armstrong	98

Preface

Halifax is more than a place on the map - it's a living story written by ocean winds, historic streets, and the laughter of families who call it home. I was born here, and I've lived here my entire life. Over the years, I've watched Halifax grow and change, yet its soul has always remained steady - *maritime warmth, community spirit, and a deep respect for history and the sea.*

This pocket guide was created not just to list attractions, but to help readers *feel* Halifax. From the waterfront's salty air to the cobblestone whispers of history on Argyle Street, there's a rhythm to this city that draws people in and never quite lets go.

My goal is to share both the famous highlights and the hidden gems - *the kind of places locals love just as much as visitors do.* Whether you're exploring as a first-time traveler or rediscovering old favorites, I hope this book helps you connect more deeply with what makes Halifax the heart of the East Coast.

Acknowledgments

Writing this guide has been a labor of love inspired by a lifetime spent in Halifax. I owe deep gratitude to the local historians, guides, and small business owners who keep our city's stories alive day after day. To the many families who welcomed me into their communities and shared insights from Bedford to Peggy's Cove - *thank you for reminding me that hospitality is Halifax's truest landmark.*

A special thank-you to my readers and fellow travelers. Your curiosity and appreciation for authentic, mindful travel make projects like this possible. May this book lead you toward discovery, laughter, and lasting memories here on our beautiful coast.

Welcome to Halifax

There's something about Halifax that feels instantly familiar, even to first-time visitors. Maybe it's the salt-tinged air drifting in from the harbor, the sound of gulls overhead, or the steady rhythm of waves brushing against the boardwalk pilings. Maybe it's the laughter that spills from patios on a summer evening, or the music that drifts down from pubs where fiddles, guitars, and good company meet. Halifax, the capital of Nova Scotia and the beating heart of Atlantic Canada, is a city that welcomes you like a neighbor.

Families find comfort here because Halifax manages to be both energetic and relaxed, historic yet modern, small enough to feel personal but big enough to always surprise you. Its blend of coastal beauty, maritime heritage, and easygoing friendliness makes it one of Canada's most rewarding destinations - *and one that reveals itself best when explored slowly, with curiosity and a sense of adventure.*

The Heart of Atlantic Canada

Set along one of the world's largest natural harbors, Halifax has long been more than a city - *it's been a crossroads.* For centuries, it has connected people, cultures, and stories from across the Atlantic world. Its port, deeply tied to both Canada's history and its modern economy, remains the lifeblood of the region. But beyond the ships, cranes, and sea breeze, there's another pulse - *that of its people.*

Nova Scotians are known for their warmth and wit, and Halifax is where that maritime charm shines brightest. It's a city built on community, a place where strangers still nod hello on the sidewalk, where small cafés remember your order, and where kids can explore waterfront museums or splash in urban fountains while parents enjoy a coffee with a view.

While much of Atlantic Canada has a slower, rural rhythm, Halifax balances that coastal pace with urban energy. It's a city of students and sailors, artists and entrepreneurs, military traditions and maritime music. Every visitor can find a piece of themselves here, whether you're wandering historic Citadel Hill, watching ferries cross the harbor, or simply breathing in that unmistakable scent of ocean air.

To experience Halifax is to feel the spirit of Nova Scotia itself - *openhearted, resilient, and forever tied to the sea.*

The Spirit of the Harbor - Culture, Community, and Coastal Life

Everything in Halifax comes back to the harbor. It shapes the city's geography, defines its skyline, and fuels its culture. The waterfront is where locals gather, where history lingers, and where the city's maritime soul is most alive.

Take a stroll along the **Halifax Boardwalk**, and you'll understand why it's one of Canada's most beloved urban waterfronts. It stretches for several kilometers, lined with local shops, museums, markets, and restaurants. Kids love the wave-shaped playgrounds, while adults can sip locally brewed cider or grab fresh seafood straight off the pier. Street performers, musicians, and the smell of salt air create a constant sense of celebration - but one that feels friendly rather than flashy.

Across the harbor, the community of **Dartmouth** mirrors that energy in its own way. Once a separate city and now part of the Halifax Regional Municipality, Dartmouth has grown into a hub of creativity, coffee culture, and lakeside living. Families often hop aboard the harbor ferry for the short trip across the water, one of the most scenic public transit rides in the country.

Halifax's connection to the sea runs deeper than recreation or scenery. Its identity is built upon the ocean's ebb and flow. The fishing fleets, shipyards, and naval bases have long defined its economy. The sound of foghorns and the sight of lighthouses still stir something deeply Canadian in the heart of every visitor.

Yet today, Halifax has evolved beyond its maritime roots while keeping them close. You'll find world-class universities, vibrant arts communities, and a thriving culinary scene alongside centuries-old naval traditions. The result is a city that feels timeless - *proud of its past but eager for what's next.*

How to Use This Guide

This pocket guide was created with families in mind - parents, grandparents, kids, and anyone who enjoys discovering a destination together. Halifax is one of those rare cities that truly caters to all ages. You can climb a historic fortress in the morning, visit an interactive science museum in the afternoon, and end the day watching sailboats drift by the harbor at sunset.

Each chapter in this book focuses on a different part of Halifax or a specific theme. Within those pages, you'll find:

- **Highlights and Attractions:** The must-see spots that capture Halifax's essence - from the waterfront to coastal day trips.
- **Family Activities:** Parks, playgrounds, hands-on museums, and easy hikes perfect for children and teens.
- **Food & Flavor:** Family-friendly restaurants, local treats, and a taste of Halifax's growing food scene.
- **Local Tips:** Where to find parking, budget-friendly activities, and seasonal events worth timing your visit around.
- **Soft History:** Each chapter concludes with a short historical reflection that brings context and depth to what you've just read - *connecting Halifax's present-day charm to its fascinating past.*

You can read the book front to back or skip to the sections that interest you most. Think of it as your personal travel companion - *a local's insight blended with the warmth of a family guide.*

Travel Tips — Making the Most of Your Visit

Halifax is a year-round destination, but its **best season for family travel** is between **late May and early October**, when temperatures are mild, daylight is long, and the waterfront comes alive with festivals. Summer brings lively patios, farmers' markets, and boat tours, while autumn offers crisp air, golden parks, and fewer crowds.

- **Spring (April–June):** Cool and fresh, with blooming gardens and the first outdoor events of the year. Perfect for walking tours and photography.
- **Summer (July–August):** Warm but rarely hot, with average highs around 22°C (72°F). Beaches, concerts, and open-air dining dominate the season.
- **Autumn (September–October):** Halifax's most photogenic months - fall foliage, harvest festivals, and cozy evenings by the water.
- **Winter (November–March):** Quieter, but magical for those who enjoy snow-dusted cityscapes, indoor museums, and local theater.

Weather Tip: Halifax's maritime climate means it can change quickly. Layered clothing and comfortable shoes are key. Always keep a light jacket handy - *even on sunny days, that ocean breeze can surprise you!*

Family Accommodation Zones

For families, location makes all the difference - and Halifax offers several neighborhoods that combine convenience, comfort, and character.

- **Downtown Halifax:** The best choice for first-time visitors. You'll be within walking distance of the waterfront, restaurants, and attractions. Hotels and short-term rentals here range from boutique inns to major chains. Great for families who want to be in the center of it all.

- **South End:** A quiet, residential area near universities and parks. Ideal for families seeking peaceful streets and green spaces like Point Pleasant Park.
- **Dartmouth Waterfront:** Just a ferry ride from downtown, Dartmouth offers a growing selection of hotels and Airbnb options - *often at lower rates*. Its lakes, markets, and playgrounds make it especially family-friendly.
- **Bedford & Sackville:** Located northwest of the downtown core, these suburbs are ideal for extended stays or larger family groups. You'll find budget-friendly hotels, shopping centers, and quick access to the highway for day trips.
- **Coastal Communities (Prospect Bay, Eastern Passage):** For families who want ocean views and a quieter retreat, these areas combine small-town charm with easy access to Halifax proper.

Getting Around

Halifax is compact enough that you can explore most major attractions without a car - especially if you're staying downtown. The waterfront boardwalk, Citadel Hill, and public gardens are all within easy walking distance. The ferry system connects you to Dartmouth, while buses and ride-shares make it easy to reach outlying areas.

For day trips, like Peggy's Cove or Lawrencetown Beach, renting a car is recommended. The scenic drives are a highlight of visiting Nova Scotia, and most are well-marked with the province's signature blue tourism signs.

Pro Tip: *If you're visiting with children, the Halifax Transit ferry ride is both practical and entertaining - it's one of the most affordable harbor tours you can take.*

Orientation - Understanding the Halifax Region

When most people think of Halifax, they picture the bustling downtown and its famous harbourfront. But the **Halifax Regional Municipality (HRM)** stretches far beyond the city's historic core, encompassing over 5,000 square kilometers of coastline, lakes, and forest. Understanding the region helps you plan a richer, more varied trip.

- **Halifax Peninsula:** The city's historic heart, where you'll find the Citadel, waterfront, and many of the main attractions. Compact, walk-able, and full of charm.
- **Dartmouth:** Across the harbor, known for its lakes, markets, and vibrant arts scene. The ferry ride itself is part of the adventure.
- **Bedford:** A suburban community along the Bedford Basin, known for family-friendly parks, shops, and scenic views.
- **Sackville:** Residential and relaxed, with easy access to hiking trails and outdoor recreation.
- **Coastal Communities:** From **Peggy's Cove** in the west to **Eastern Passage** in the east, the smaller coastal villages provide classic maritime scenery - *lighthouses, fishing boats, and seaside cafés.*

Each area has its own personality, and together they make Halifax more than just a city - it's a collection of communities woven together by water, culture, and pride.

From Fortress to Cultural Capital

Halifax's story begins in **1749**, when British settlers established a fortified town along the natural harbor. Its strategic location - *midway between Europe and North America* - made it a vital naval base and trading port. Wooden ships, redcoat soldiers, and merchants filled the early streets, building a settlement that would become the cornerstone of British power in Atlantic Canada.

But Halifax was never just a military outpost. From the beginning, it attracted people from many backgrounds - *Indigenous Mi'kmaq communities, Acadian families, African Nova Scotians, and immigrants from across Europe.* The city grew with the sea as its anchor: shipbuilding, fishing, and naval defense were the threads that wove its early life together.

The **Halifax Explosion of 1917** - *one of the largest non-nuclear explosions in history* - devastated much of the city but also revealed the strength of its people. The global outpouring of aid, particularly from Boston, forged a bond that still endures today. Halifax rebuilt stronger and prouder, becoming a city that honors its history without being defined by it.

Today, Halifax stands as a modern cultural capital - *home to universities, museums, festivals, and a thriving creative scene.* Yet, even as glass towers rise along the waterfront, the echoes of the past remain. You can still hear the cannon fire from Citadel Hill each noon, walk the cobblestones laid by early settlers, or stand at the harbor's edge and imagine the tall ships that once filled its waters.

Halifax has always been a city in motion - forward-looking yet rooted in its maritime soul. For visitors, that balance between old and new, tradition and innovation, is what makes it so captivating.

Final Thoughts – Beginning Your Journey

As you prepare to explore Halifax, remember that this city is best enjoyed at a walking pace. Stop for an ice cream by the water, chat with locals, let the kids feed the ducks in the Public Gardens, or watch the fog roll in from the Atlantic. Every corner has a story, every neighborhood its own rhythm.

Whether you're here for a weekend or a week, you'll soon understand why Halifax is known as "where Nova Scotia's heart meets the sea." It's more than a slogan - it's a truth you feel the moment you arrive.

The Historic Waterfront

A Stroll Through Time and Tide

There's a rhythm to the Halifax waterfront that's unlike anywhere else in Canada. It's the sound of gulls and ship horns echoing across the harbor, the creak of mooring ropes, and the chatter of visitors as they follow the boardwalk's curve along the water's edge. The Halifax waterfront isn't just a tourist attraction - *it's the living, beating heart of the city.*

Stretching more than four kilometers from Pier 21 to Casino Nova Scotia, this wooden boardwalk is a stage for Nova Scotia's maritime soul. You'll find buskers strumming guitars beside floating restaurants, sea captains swapping stories near the tall ships, and families pausing for an ice cream while watching ferries drift between the Halifax and Dartmouth skylines.

Whether you come for history, seafood, or the salt air, the waterfront is where Halifax truly reveals itself - part working harbor, part open-air museum, and part playground by the sea.

The Halifax Boardwalk: Key Stops

The boardwalk is designed to be explored slowly. Most visitors begin at **Queen's Marque**, a stunning modern development that blends architecture with Atlantic storytelling. Here, art installations and interpretive panels celebrate the city's connection to the sea. The open plaza, facing the harbor, is alive with families dipping toes into shallow water features, couples enjoying patio cocktails, and children chasing bubbles carried by ocean breeze.

From Queen's Marque, follow the boardwalk north and you'll reach the **Salt Yard**, one of the most vibrant spots on the waterfront. A cluster of brightly painted kiosks offers everything from handmade crafts and Nova Scotia T-shirts to lobster rolls and saltwater taffy. On summer weekends, the area hums with music and laughter. It's the perfect place to pick up a souvenir or simply people-watch with a cone of local *Cows Ice Cream* - a Halifax staple that's as much a tradition as it is a treat.

Continue along the boardwalk to **Cable Wharf**, a hub of harbor adventure. This historic wharf was once a key communications link for transatlantic telegraph cables, connecting North America to Europe under the sea. Today, the wharf has been reimagined as a launch point for boat tours, dining, and family fun. Murphy's at the Cable Wharf offers fresh seafood with panoramic water views—an ideal stop for lunch before setting out to explore the harbor from the water.

Maritime Museum of the Atlantic

Few museums capture the essence of a city the way the **Maritime Museum of the Atlantic** does for Halifax. Located right on the waterfront, this museum tells stories that are as powerful as the tides themselves.

The exhibits take visitors deep into the maritime world - *from heroic rescues and shipwrecks to the daily life of sailors who braved the Atlantic.* One of the most moving displays is the section dedicated to the **Titanic**. Halifax played a unique role in the aftermath of the disaster; ships from the city were dispatched to recover victims from the icy waters. Personal artifacts, like a child's shoes and ship fragments, create a human connection to history that lingers long after you leave.

You'll also find a fascinating exhibit on the **Halifax Explosion of 1917**, one of the most catastrophic events in Canadian history. A French munitions ship, *Mont-Blanc*, collided with another vessel in the harbor, setting off an explosion that leveled much of the city. More than 1,900 people lost their lives, and thousands more were injured. The museum's "Explosion Bell" rings in remembrance of that day - *a powerful symbol of Halifax's resilience.*

For families, the museum's hands-on exhibits - ***miniature ship models, knot-tying stations, and navigation tools*** - turn learning into adventure.

Kids can climb aboard a real deck section and feel what it's like to be part of a crew, steering toward discovery.

Harbor Tours and Tall Ships

Seeing Halifax from the water is like looking at a portrait painted from the artist's true perspective. The harbor defines the city - it's both the backdrop and the reason Halifax exists. Fortunately, there are plenty of ways to experience it up close.

Murphy's the Cable Wharf offers several popular options, from leisurely sightseeing cruises to themed adventures. The **Harbor Hopper**, an amphibious vehicle that doubles as both a bus and a boat, is one of Halifax's most beloved family attractions. The tour begins on land, driving through historic streets before splashing directly into the harbor. The mix of humor, local trivia, and splashing fun makes it a hit with kids and adults alike.

For something a little more romantic or traditional, tall ship tours aboard vessels like the **Silva** or **Mar** offer a taste of 18th-century sailing life. The creak of wooden masts and the smell of sea salt instantly transport you to another era. Sunset cruises are particularly magical, with the skyline bathed in gold and the lighthouse at Georges Island casting its steady beam.

If you'd prefer to explore at your own pace, consider renting a kayak or taking the **Halifax-Dartmouth Ferry,** one of the oldest saltwater ferry services in the world. For just a few dollars, you can glide across the harbor, enjoy sweeping city views, and step into Dartmouth's growing waterfront district.

Best Family Dining Along the Waterfront

Halifax is known for its seafood, and the waterfront offers some of the freshest catches anywhere in Canada. But it's also full of casual, family-friendly spots that make dining easy for travelers with kids in tow.

The Bicycle Thief remains a favorite for both locals and visitors, combining Italian-inspired comfort food with unbeatable harbor views. The patio fills up quickly in summer, where guests linger over pasta and local wine while boats drift by just meters away.

For a laid-back meal, **Pickford & Black** offers classic seafood dishes - *think fish tacos, mussels, and chowder* - in a space that balances maritime tradition with a modern twist. Families often gather here for early dinners, with plenty of kid-friendly options and a warm maritime vibe.

Those looking for something quick and fun should stop by the **Salt Yard**'s food stalls. Grab fish and chips, lobster rolls, or freshly squeezed lemonade and enjoy an impromptu picnic by the boardwalk. Of course, no visit is complete without a stop at **Cows Ice Cream** - *voted one of the best ice creams in the world by Reader's Digest*. The playful cow-themed flavors and hand-made cones are a hit with kids and adults alike.

For those seeking a memorable night out, **Waterfront Warehouse** combines maritime heritage and fine dining in one elegant space, set inside a former cold storage building. Fresh oysters, Atlantic salmon, and scallops are menu highlights - *true tastes of Nova Scotia's sea bounty*.

Halifax Fun Facts -

- The **Halifax Harbor** is the **second-largest natural harbor in the world**, after Sydney, Australia.
- The **Harbor Hopper** began life as an amphibious military vehicle before being repurposed for tourism.
- **Queen's Marque** means "Queen's Brand" in old English - reflecting Halifax's historic link to the Crown.
- The **Explosion Bell** at the Maritime Museum is rung each year on December 6th in memory of the 1917 Halifax Explosion.
- Halifax's boardwalk is one of the **longest downtown boardwalks in the world**, stretching over four kilometers.
- The **Halifax-Dartmouth Ferry**, established in 1752, is the **oldest continuously running saltwater ferry service** in North America.

How Halifax's Harbor Shaped Its Destiny

Halifax owes its existence - *and much of its character* - to its magnificent harbor. When the British founded the settlement in **1749**, they chose this location for its deep, ice-free waters and naturally sheltered shape. The site was ideal for a naval stronghold, designed to counter French influence in the region and protect British interests in North America.

The city's early history was one of strategic importance and constant growth. Massive stone fortifications like **Citadel Hill** rose above the harbor, and the docks below became vital for ship repair, trade, and military operations. During both World Wars, Halifax was Canada's naval command center, where convoys gathered before crossing the Atlantic under the threat of German submarines.

As the centuries passed, the harbor transitioned from a fortress zone to a gateway of trade and immigration. Ships carrying settlers, soldiers, and supplies arrived by the thousands, each wave of newcomers leaving an imprint on the city's culture. The harbor became a place of welcome and remembrance - *its waters reflecting both triumph and tragedy.*

By the late 20th century, the waterfront had evolved again, this time into a cultural hub celebrating Halifax's maritime heritage rather than its military one. Historic warehouses were reborn as museums, restaurants, and artisan shops. The once-industrial piers became gathering spaces for locals and visitors alike.

Family Travel Tips – The Halifax Waterfront

- **Best Time to Visit:** Mornings are peaceful for stroller walks and photography, while afternoons bring lively crowds and street performers. Summer evenings often feature live music, especially near Queen's Marque and Salt Yard.
- **Parking:** Metered and paid parking can be found along Lower Water Street and at the Waterfront Parking Lot near Bishop's Landing. Consider leaving the car in a downtown parkade and walking the full boardwalk.
- **Accessibility:** The entire boardwalk is stroller and wheelchair-friendly, with ramps and wide wooden planks throughout. Many restaurants offer highchairs and kid-friendly menus.
- **Budget Tip:** Take the **Halifax-Dartmouth Ferry** for a scenic harbor experience at a fraction of the cost of a private cruise. Kids under 12 ride free on most Metro Transit routes.
- **Rainy Day Alternative:** The **Maritime Museum of the Atlantic** and the **Discovery Center** (a few blocks uphill on Lower Water Street) are excellent indoor attractions for curious young explorers.
- **Snack Breaks:** Cows Ice Cream, Beavertails, and the Salt Yard food

stalls make perfect stops between sightseeing.

Today, Halifax's harbor remains central to the city's identity, not just as a geographical landmark, but as a symbol of resilience, renewal, and community. From naval battles to festivals, from shipyards to sailing tours, the harbor continues to shape the city's story, just as it has for nearly three centuries.

This is where Halifax's history meets horizon - where the heart of Halifax beats in time with the sea.

Downtown Discoveries

If the waterfront is Halifax's handshake, then its downtown core is the heartbeat - *a lively mix of historic charm, creative energy, and community warmth.* The moment you step uphill from the harbor, cobblestones give way to bustling city streets lined with cafés, shops, and green spaces. Downtown Halifax offers something for everyone - from children chasing ducks in the park to parents sipping lattes beside blooming gardens, to families discovering stories of soldiers, sailors, and scholars who helped shape the city's past and present.

Spring Garden Road and the Public Gardens

No visit to downtown Halifax is complete without a stroll along **Spring Garden Road**, a vibrant street that perfectly captures the city's youthful yet historic character. Known as Halifax's main shopping and cultural artery, it's lined with independent boutiques, bookstores, local fashion labels, and cozy cafés that spill out onto the sidewalks in summer. The scent of roasted coffee drifts through the air, mingling with the sweet floral notes carried up from the **Halifax Public Gardens**, located just a few steps away.

The **Halifax Public Gardens** are a masterpiece of Victorian-era landscaping, carefully manicured flowerbeds, wrought-iron gates, meandering gravel paths, and elegant fountains all evoke a sense of 19th-century tranquility. Families will find the gardens ideal for a peaceful break amid the bustle of downtown. Kids can watch ducks glide across the pond, parents can sit on shaded benches, and together they can admire the intricate floral arrangements that change with the seasons.

In summer, the gardens' **bandstand** hosts free afternoon concerts - *a perfect way to slow down and soak in the old-fashioned charm.* Grab a lemonade from a nearby vendor, find a patch of grass beneath a chestnut tree, and enjoy the music floating through the park. The gardens close at dusk, but during daylight hours they feel timeless, as if Halifax's modern city life pauses briefly at the gates.

Just outside the gardens, you'll find an array of cafés and lunch spots catering to all tastes, from gourmet sandwiches and vegetarian fare to kid-friendly pizza and ice cream shops. It's one of those places where you can spend a leisurely morning exploring, stop for a meal, and then wander into the next adventure without needing to plan ahead.

The Halifax Central Library – Modern Architecture Meets Community Spirit

At first glance, the **Halifax Central Library** looks unlike anything else in the city. Its modern, glass-clad design - *resembling a stack of books tilted in motion* - has become one of Halifax's architectural icons since opening in 2014. Inside, it's more than a library; it's a hub for learning, play, and creativity that perfectly embodies Halifax's community-oriented spirit.

Families will find the **children's floor** a highlight. Bright, colorful, and full of cozy nooks for reading, it's designed to spark curiosity and imagination. There are interactive play areas for toddlers, storytime sessions, and shelves filled with picture books from around the world. For older kids, there's a tech zone with computers, creative labs, and even occasional workshops for digital design or crafts.

Parents, meanwhile, often gravitate to the top floor, home to the **rooftop terrace**, offering panoramic views over the city skyline and Citadel Hill. The in-house café serves excellent coffee and pastries, making it one of the most relaxing spots in downtown Halifax to pause and take in the view.

The Central Library stands as a modern reflection of what Halifax values most - learning, inclusivity, and gathering places where all ages can feel at home. Whether you stop in for a few minutes or spend a whole afternoon, it's a destination that blends education with enjoyment in a way few libraries manage to do.

Citadel Hill – Echoes of the Past

Standing guard above downtown, **Halifax Citadel National Historic Site** is impossible to miss. Its star-shaped fort rises from the center of the city, a reminder of the days when Halifax was a vital military stronghold protecting Britain's interests in North America. Today, it's one of the city's most visited attractions - *and a surprisingly fun experience for families.*

Step through the gates, and you're transported to the 1800s. Costumed soldiers patrol the ramparts, fifes and drums echo through the air, and kids can watch (or jump at) the **noon cannon firing**, a tradition that has continued almost daily since 1857. Inside, the **Army Museum** offers fascinating exhibits on uniforms, weaponry, and local military history, but the real joy lies in the interactive experiences: children can try on period uniforms, participate in mock drills, and chat with the staff who reenact life in the barracks.

The **view from the Citadel's ramparts** is unmatched, stretching across the downtown core, the harbor, and Dartmouth beyond. It's an ideal photo spot, especially around sunset when the city glows gold beneath the sky.

For a deeper sense of connection, consider timing your visit with one of the fort's special events. The **Ghost Tours** held in the evenings mix storytelling with history, while summer festivals often bring live music and family-friendly programming to the grounds. The Citadel is part of Halifax's living history - *not just a monument, but a space where past and present meet in a uniquely engaging way.*

DOWNTOWN DISCOVERIES

Family Cafés, Bookstores, and Rainy-Day Ideas

Halifax is famous for its unpredictable weather - *sunshine one moment, mist the next* - but that never stops the fun. Downtown offers a variety of cozy indoor escapes perfect for a drizzly day.

Book lovers should visit **Bookmark Halifax**, an independent bookstore on Spring Garden Road that's a treasure trove of regional literature and travel guides. For families, the nearby **Tattamagouche Ice Creamery** and **Humani-T Café** offer sweet treats and creative spaces where kids can draw, read, or people-watch from the windows.

If you're visiting on a rainy morning, the **Discovery Center** on Lower Water Street is only a short walk away, a modern science museum filled with hands-on exhibits that encourage kids to explore physics, technology, and the natural world. It's a fantastic way to blend fun and learning while staying dry.

For something more relaxed, consider an afternoon at **The Biscuit General Store** - *a quirky local shop mixing retro charm and family-friendly browsing* - or grab a movie at the **Cineplex Park Lane**, located just off Spring Garden. With everything within walking distance, downtown Halifax proves that even a gray day can become a memorable adventure.

Family Tips -

- **Best Time to Explore:** Mornings are quieter for shopping and sightseeing; afternoons bring livelier crowds and performances, especially around Spring Garden and Citadel Hill.
- **Rainy-Day Alternatives:** The Central Library and Discovery

Center make perfect indoor stops. Many cafés along Spring Garden are stroller-friendly and offer children's menus.
- **Transportation Tip:** Downtown is compact - walking is the best way to explore. Street parking can be tight, so consider parking once and exploring on foot.
- **Budget Idea:** Admission to the Halifax Public Gardens is free year-round, and entry to Citadel Hill is free for kids under 17 when accompanied by an adult.
- **Snack Stops:** Try Cows Ice Cream near Spring Garden or the rooftop café inside the library for city views and treats.
- **Family Photo Spot:** The Citadel's ramparts offer panoramic views of the city and harbor, perfect for a memorable vacation snapshot.

Fun Facts -

- The **noon gun** has fired from Citadel Hill nearly every day since 1857 - *one of the longest-running traditions of its kind in North America.*
- The **Halifax Public Gardens** are among the oldest formal Victorian gardens in North America, established in 1867, the same year Canada became a country.
- The **Halifax Central Library's** design was inspired by the image of books stacked on a shelf - *symbolizing knowledge, community, and imagination.*

A Stroll Through Time

In many ways, downtown Halifax grew outward from the Citadel. The hill once watched over a town of narrow streets and wooden houses that bustled with merchants, sailors, and soldiers. From its founding in 1749, Halifax was built to protect the British Empire's interests in the North Atlantic, and the Citadel stood as its heart of defense.

But as wars ended and peace settled, the city began to reinvent itself. Spring Garden Road emerged from farmland into a lively commercial district. The public gardens became a symbol of Victorian civility and leisure - *a place where citizens could walk among flowers instead of fortifications.* The modern skyline, crowned by the shimmering glass of the Central Library, now represents progress and openness rather than protection and isolation.

Through all its changes, the downtown area has retained something essential - *resilience*. The Citadel still fires its cannon each day as a salute not just to the past, but to a city that continues to evolve with optimism and pride.

From the echo of the gun to the laughter of children in the gardens below, Halifax's downtown tells a story of endurance, growth, and the enduring beauty of community.

Dartmouth: Across the Harbor

Across the sparkling expanse of Halifax Harbor lies a community with a rhythm all its own - **Dartmouth**, affectionately known as "the City of Lakes." Though often viewed as Halifax's quieter counterpart, Dartmouth is brimming with creativity, family fun, and outdoor beauty. It's a place where waterfront walks meet lakeside paddles, where local markets buzz with handmade crafts, and where every café seems to know your name.

For families, crossing the harbor to Dartmouth feels like stepping into

DARTMOUTH: ACROSS THE HARBOR

a relaxed, small-town retreat while staying within sight of Halifax's skyline. Whether you take the ferry across or drive the bridge, Dartmouth rewards curious travelers with its blend of local pride and unhurried charm.

Crossing the Harbor – The Halifax-Dartmouth Ferry

Before highways and bridges, ferries were the lifelines connecting Halifax to the communities across the water. Today, the **Halifax-Dartmouth ferry** remains one of the oldest continuously operating saltwater ferry services in North America - *a tradition dating back to 1752.*

Boarding the ferry feels like part of the adventure. The journey lasts only about 10 minutes, but it offers some of the best views of both skylines. As the ferry glides out from Halifax's terminal, you'll see the Citadel perched proudly above the city, ships passing through the harbor, and seagulls wheeling overhead. On clear mornings, the light sparkles off the water, and at sunset, the skyline glows in gold and rose hues - *a photographer's delight.*

Kids love the novelty of the ferry ride, sitting up top, feeling the wind in their hair, and watching the city shrink behind them. Parents will appreciate how convenient and affordable it is: it's part of the city's **Metro Transit** network, so the same passes or transfers used on buses apply here. If you time it right, you can enjoy a return journey in the evening, when Halifax's waterfront lights shimmer like stars across the bay.

Arriving at the **Alderney Landing terminal** puts you right in the heart of Dartmouth's waterfront, within walking distance of markets, cafés, and lake trails.

Alderney Landing – Culture, Markets, and Local Flavor

Stepping off the ferry, your first stop should be **Alderney Landing**, a community hub that blends art, local food, and family entertainment. The **Alderney Farmers' Market**, held on Saturdays, is one of the best in the region, featuring fresh produce, baked goods, local honey, and handmade crafts. It's a lively, colorful scene where locals gather for breakfast sandwiches, coffee, and friendly chatter.

Throughout the year, Alderney Landing also hosts festivals, concerts, and seasonal events like **Canada Day celebrations**, **Christmas markets**, and **outdoor movie nights**. The **Alderney Theater** often features performances from local artists and youth theater groups - a great way to experience Nova Scotia's creative community.

Just behind the complex, a **playground and open plaza** offer plenty of space for kids to burn off energy while parents enjoy harbor views. Nearby, you'll find casual dining options with outdoor patios and walk-up windows serving everything from tacos to lobster rolls. It's the perfect spot to spend a few relaxed hours before venturing farther into Dartmouth's lake district.

Lake Banook and Lake Micmac – The City of Lakes in Action

If Halifax has the ocean, Dartmouth has its lakes - *23 of them, in fact*. Among these, **Lake Banook** and **Lake Micmac** are the most famous and easily accessible from downtown. Both lakes offer a blend of recreation and relaxation, ideal for families looking to swim, paddle, or simply picnic by the water.

DARTMOUTH: ACROSS THE HARBOR

Lake Banook, just a few minutes from Alderney Landing, has earned international recognition as a world-class paddling venue. Its calm waters have hosted canoe and kayak championships for decades, and local clubs still practice here daily. Families can rent paddle-boards or kayaks in summer, or simply sit along the lake's edge watching the boats glide by. The **Banook Canoe Club** occasionally offers beginner lessons and kids' camps, giving young adventurers a chance to try something new.

Nearby, **Lake Micmac** offers a quieter setting with forested trails and the **Shubie Park** greenway connecting the lakes. Shubie Park is one of Dartmouth's gems - a sprawling urban park with walking and cycling trails, picnic areas, and interpretive signs that trace the route of the historic **Shubenacadie Canal**. It's a great spot for a family walk, with opportunities to spot ducks, turtles, and the occasional heron along the water's edge.

On warm summer afternoons, locals gather at **Birch Cove Beach** on Lake Banook or **Micmac Beach** for swimming and sandcastle building. There are lifeguards on duty during the main season, change rooms, and snack kiosks nearby. For families visiting in cooler months, the lakes still hold their charm - *perfect for a brisk lakeside walk or watching paddlers cut through morning mist.*

Graffiti, Murals, and Quirky Cafés

Dartmouth has undergone a creative renaissance over the past decade. Once a quiet residential suburb, it's now a vibrant arts community filled with murals, indie shops, and some of the best cafés in the Halifax Regional Municipality.

A walk through downtown Dartmouth reveals splashes of color at every turn. **Graffiti murals** adorn building walls, depicting everything from maritime history to local folklore. These murals, part of community art initiatives, have turned the town's streets into an open-air gallery that delights both kids and adults. One of the most photographed is the **Underwater Mural** near Portland Street, featuring whimsical sea creatures painted by local artists.

When you're ready for a break, Dartmouth's café scene does not disappoint. **Two If By Sea**, a local favorite near the ferry terminal, is famous for its over-sized croissants and welcoming atmosphere. Families will find plenty of space and a friendly vibe that encourages you to linger. For something sweet, **Portland Street Crêperie** serves dessert and breakfast crêpes with generous portions that satisfy every age group.

For those who love browsing unique finds, **Kept Gift Shop** and **New Scotland Clothing Co.** both celebrate Nova Scotia's creativity and coastal identity. These small businesses often collaborate with local artists, and many carry kid-friendly souvenirs, handmade toys, and maritime-themed gifts perfect for taking home.

A Walk Through Downtown Dartmouth

Beyond its cafés and markets, downtown Dartmouth invites exploration on foot. The area is compact, pedestrian-friendly, and full of unexpected discoveries. You might stumble upon a **tiny free library** tucked beside a mural, or a musician playing guitar on a bench near King's Wharf.

Ochterloney Street and **Portland Street** are the main arteries, lined with boutique shops, restaurants, and bakeries. Families can stroll

DARTMOUTH: ACROSS THE HARBOR

from Alderney Landing to the lakefront in less than 20 minutes, passing through a mix of heritage homes and newer developments that showcase Dartmouth's growth.

In recent years, **King's Wharf** has transformed the waterfront with modern condos, restaurants, and a scenic boardwalk. From here, you can gaze back at Halifax across the water - *a stunning reminder of how close yet distinct the two cities are.*

Family Tips -

- **Best Way to Get There:** Take the ferry from Halifax's Lower Water Street terminal to Alderney Landing. The ride is quick, scenic, and affordable - *and fun for kids.*
- **Best Time to Visit:** Saturday mornings are perfect for the Alderney Market, while summer afternoons are great for lakeside fun and outdoor dining.
- **Getting Around:** Most downtown attractions are walk-able. For exploring the lakes, renting bikes or using public transit is easy and inexpensive.
- **Budget Tip:** The ferry fare is included with a Metro Transit transfer, and kids under 12 often ride free. Shubie Park trails and beaches are free year-round.
- **Snack Spots:** Try *Two If By Sea* for croissants, Portland Street Crêperie for a treat, or stop by Alderney Landing's market stalls for local goodies.
- **Photo Opportunities:** Capture the Halifax skyline from Alderney Landing, or the colorful paddle-boards gliding across Lake Banook.

Fun Facts -

- The **Halifax–Dartmouth ferry** is one of the oldest continuously operating saltwater ferry routes in North America, established in 1752.
- Dartmouth is nicknamed the **"City of Lakes"** for its 23 natural lakes, many of which are swimmable and interconnected by trails.
- The **Shubenacadie Canal**, portions of which run through Dartmouth, was originally built in the 1820s to connect Halifax Harbor with the Bay of Fundy.
- **Two If By Sea Café** operates out of a converted fire station and is known for some of the largest croissants in Atlantic Canada.

From Independence to Integration

Dartmouth's story is one of transformation - *from a small, independent settlement to an essential part of greater Halifax's identity.* Founded in 1750, just a year after Halifax, it was originally established as a home for British settlers seeking farmland across the harbor. But life in early Dartmouth was harsh; the community endured repeated hardships, including raids during conflicts with the Mi'kmaq and French forces.

Over time, Dartmouth grew into a thriving industrial and shipbuilding town. Its sawmills, foundries, and wharves played a crucial role in Nova Scotia's economy. By the late 19th century, it had developed its own civic pride and governance, remaining independent from Halifax for more than two centuries.

That independence officially ended in **1996**, when Dartmouth merged with Halifax and several surrounding communities to form the **Halifax Regional Municipality (HRM)**. While some residents were initially reluctant, the merger allowed for shared resources, coordinated development, and a unified regional identity.

Yet Dartmouth never lost its character. Today, it stands proudly as a distinct community within the HRM, creative, community-driven, and deeply connected to its natural surroundings.

Crossing the harbor now means more than just a short ferry ride; it's a passage between two halves of one vibrant whole, each reflecting the other across the shimmering waters of Halifax Harbor.

Point Pleasant Park and the South End

A Coastal Haven in the City

Few places capture the quiet beauty of Halifax like **Point Pleasant Park**, a 190-acre green sanctuary tucked at the city's southern tip. It's a place where families come to unwind, locals bring their dogs for a run beneath the pines, and visitors get their first real sense of how the ocean defines life in this harbor city. The air is heavy with salt and spruce; gulls glide overhead as the waves break gently against the rocky shore.

Point Pleasant isn't just a park - *it's a local tradition*. On any sunny weekend, the park's winding trails fill with joggers, parents pushing strollers, children on bikes, and university students escaping the buzz of downtown. The well-maintained pathways lead through quiet woodlands and open meadows to stunning lookout points across the **Northwest Arm** and **Halifax Harbor**. Benches and picnic tables are scattered throughout, inviting visitors to stay a while and enjoy the ever-changing maritime views.

Walking Trails and Fort Ruins

One of the best ways to explore Point Pleasant Park is simply to wander. The network of trails - *more than 39 in total* - offers everything from leisurely strolls to brisk coastal hikes. Families with young children will appreciate the level, stroller-friendly main paths like **Shakespeare by the Sea Trail**, while more adventurous walkers can branch off onto narrower forest tracks leading to old fortifications and scenic overlooks.

Scattered throughout the park are the **stone remnants of 18th- and 19th-century British defenses**, reminders of a time when Halifax was a critical military post. Among the most notable ruins is **Fort Ogilvie**, built in 1793 to defend against potential French attack, and **Prince of Wales Tower**, the oldest Martello tower in North America. The tower stands as a cylindrical stone sentinel overlooking the sea - *a silent echo of the era when the city's safety depended on vigilance and cannon fire.*

While most of the structures are now quiet and moss-covered, they spark the imagination. Kids love to climb the old embankments and peek through the narrow cannon slits, while history-minded visitors can appreciate the strategic genius of these coastal placements.

Picnics, Dogs, and Coastal Play

Point Pleasant Park is wonderfully **family- and pet-friendly**, offering plenty of space to run, play, and relax. The large **off-leash dog area** is one of the city's most popular gathering spots for pet owners, and it's common to see dogs bounding joyfully into the water along the shore.

For picnics, the **Black Rock Beach area** and the **Sailors' Memorial Walk** offer flat grassy patches with picnic tables and panoramic views. Families often pack a lunch from the nearby **South End bakeries** or cafés - try croissants from LF Bakery on South Street or sandwiches from Uncommon Grounds before heading to the park.

During summer, the park hosts **Shakespeare by the Sea**, an outdoor theater company that stages lively, family-friendly performances of classic plays amid the ruins and forests. Bring a blanket and some snacks, and you'll have one of the most magical evenings in Halifax - *live theater under the stars with ocean breezes rolling through the trees.*

The Northwest Arm and South End Charm

Leaving the park, the nearby **Northwest Arm** offers another taste of Halifax's maritime rhythm. This sheltered waterway, lined with sailboats and century-old homes, connects to the harbor and is one of the most picturesque areas in the city. You can walk the quiet **Arm Lane** trails or sit by the water's edge to watch yachts drift in and out of the Royal Nova Scotia Yacht Squadron - *the oldest yacht club in North America.*

Just beyond the park lies the **South End**, a neighborhood known for its **leafy streets, elegant Victorian homes, and university energy**. It's home to **Saint Mary's University** and **Dalhousie University**, which bring a youthful vibrancy to the otherwise genteel atmosphere. Cafés, independent bookstores, and hidden gardens make the South End a delight to explore on foot. Families often enjoy an afternoon walk from Point Pleasant Park up through **Young Avenue**, admiring the stately old houses and mature trees before stopping at **The Wired Monk Café** or **Tart & Soul Bakery** for coffee and pastries.

The South End is also ideal for those looking for quieter accommodations near downtown. Boutique inns and bed-and-breakfasts in this area give visitors the feeling of staying in a local neighborhood while remaining close to the waterfront and attractions.

The Legacy of Defense

The peaceful beauty of Point Pleasant Park belies its strategic past. Long before it became a place of leisure, these wooded slopes and rocky shores were part of a vital chain of defenses protecting Halifax Harbor.

The **British military established Point Pleasant as a fortified zone in the mid-1700s**, shortly after the city's founding. The location was ideal - its southern position allowed cannons to command both the entrance to the harbor and the Northwest Arm, ensuring that no hostile ship could approach unnoticed. Throughout the 18th and 19th centuries, multiple batteries and redoubts were built here, creating an intricate defensive network linked to Citadel Hill and George's Island.

When global conflicts waned and the threat of invasion faded, the park's military importance declined. By the late 1800s, Point Pleasant had been transformed into a **public park**, thanks to a 999-year lease from the British Crown - *famously agreed upon for a mere* **one shilling per** *year.*

Family Tips -

- **Parking:** There are two main entrances - ***Tower Road and Point Pleasant Drive*** - each with limited free parking. Arrive early on sunny weekends.
- **Best Time to Visit:** Mornings are ideal for quiet walks; evenings are perfect for catching the sunset over the Northwest Arm.
- **Accessibility:** Main trails are stroller and wheelchair friendly; side trails can be uneven.
- **Picnic Essentials:** Bring your own food - there are no concessions inside the park. Nearby cafés on South Street are great for takeout.
- **Dog-Friendly:** Off-leash areas are clearly marked; remember to bring waste bags and fresh water for pets.
- **Nearby Eats:** Try **Henry House Pub** for classic Maritime fare or **Cora's South End** for a hearty family breakfast before your park adventure.

Fun Facts -

- The land for Point Pleasant Park is leased from the **British Crown for one shilling per year**, a symbolic rent that continues today.
- **Prince of Wales Tower**, built in 1796, is **the oldest Martello tower in North America**.
- The park covers **190 acres** and contains over **39 kilometers of walking trails**.
- Point Pleasant Park's **forest was devastated by Hurricane Juan in 2003**, leading to an extensive replanting program that continues today.

Today, visitors can still trace the outlines of the old fortifications, some now reclaimed by the forest. The park stands as a living monument to Halifax's layered identity: part fortress, part forest, and wholly maritime.

Museums, Art and Science for All Ages

A City That Inspires Curiosity

Halifax isn't just a harbor city, it's a place of stories, science, and imagination. From the roar of a cannon at Citadel Hill to the hushed halls of an art gallery, there's always something that sparks wonder. Families visiting Halifax will quickly discover that this city celebrates learning in hands-on, engaging ways. Kids can climb, create, and experiment, while adults enjoy exhibits that reveal the deeper layers of

Atlantic Canada's history and culture.

Whether your family loves **art, discovery, or maritime heritage**, Halifax offers a surprising variety of museums that manage to be both educational and fun. Here, every exhibit tells part of the story of Nova Scotia - the spirit of the sea, the creativity of its people, and the resilience of communities shaped by centuries of change.

The Discovery Center – Where Science Comes Alive

At the top of the list for family travelers is the **Discovery Center**, a dynamic, interactive museum that brings science to life through play, technology, and imagination. Located on Lower Water Street, just a short walk from the waterfront, the Center's four floors are packed with hands-on exhibits, digital installations, and creative labs that make learning irresistible.

The **Wonder Gallery**, designed especially for kids under eight, is a cheerful, safe space where little ones can experiment with water tables, building blocks, and shadow play. Older children and teens gravitate toward the **Flight Gallery**, where they can test flight simulators or learn how wind and lift work through hands-on experiments. The **Health Gallery** invites families to pedal bikes to generate electricity, while the **Innovation Lab** hosts weekend workshops and science shows that change regularly.

The building itself is bright and modern, with wide open spaces and natural light streaming through floor-to-ceiling windows. Parents can relax with coffee at the small on-site café while their children explore freely in a supervised, secure environment. Families visiting Halifax in winter will especially appreciate the Discovery Center - *it's a warm, engaging refuge from chilly maritime winds and a perfect half-day outing.*

Art Gallery of Nova Scotia – Creativity by the Sea

A short walk uphill from the waterfront brings visitors to the **Art Gallery of Nova Scotia (AGNS)**, a cornerstone of the city's cultural scene. The gallery offers a welcoming introduction to Atlantic Canadian art, from historical portraits to bold contemporary installations.

For families, the highlight is often the **Maud Lewis House**, a small, brightly painted structure preserved in its entirety inside the gallery. The home of Nova Scotia's most beloved folk artist, Maud Lewis, is a burst of color and optimism - every surface is hand-painted with flowers, birds, and rural scenes. Children are instantly drawn to its joyful simplicity, and parents often find it deeply moving to stand inside the humble space where one of Canada's most iconic painters created her world.

Beyond Maud Lewis, the AGNS hosts changing exhibitions of regional, national, and Indigenous art. Family-friendly activity sheets and occasional weekend art-making sessions invite visitors to participate creatively rather than simply observe. The gallery café and gift shop are worth a stop as well, perfect for a snack and a locally inspired souvenir before continuing your downtown explorations.

Maritime Museum of the Atlantic – Halifax's Seafaring Soul

Though already introduced in the Waterfront chapter, the **Maritime Museum of the Atlantic** deserves another mention as part of Halifax's cultural trio. Its rich collection of ship models, nautical instruments, and artifacts tells the ongoing story of the sea and its deep bond with Nova Scotia.

The museum's **Titanic exhibit** is particularly compelling, connecting Halifax to one of the world's most famous maritime tragedies. The city played a key role in the recovery and burial of Titanic victims, and several artifacts - *deck chairs, personal items, and poignant letters* - reflect that connection. Kids are often fascinated by the detailed ship models and by the **hands-on knot-tying stations**, where they can test their sailor skills.

Outside, the museum's small wharf area allows visitors to step aboard heritage vessels when in season. These include the **CSS Acadia**, a hydrographic survey ship launched in 1913, and the **HMCS Sackville**, Canada's oldest surviving warship. The combination of real ships and engaging exhibits makes this a favorite for families and history enthusiasts alike.

Museum of Natural History – From the Forest to the Sea

Just uphill on Summer Street lies another local gem - *the **Museum of Natural History**, a family favorite for generations.* It's smaller and more traditional than the Discovery Center, but it carries a sense of nostalgia and charm. Exhibits cover everything from Atlantic wildlife and Mi'kmaq cultural heritage to geology and oceanography.

The museum's most famous resident is **Gus the Tortoise**, a 100-year-old gopher tortoise who has been greeting visitors since the 1940s. Gus is something of a Halifax celebrity - *his daily walks around the museum are eagerly awaited by children and staff alike.*

Other highlights include displays of Nova Scotia's natural habitats, complete with taxidermy animals and realistic dioramas, and interactive science corners where kids can learn about fossils, weather patterns, and local marine life. The museum's approachable layout and friendly staff make it an excellent stop for families seeking a calm, educational experience that still feels personal.

Pier 21 – Canada's Immigration Story

For families with older children or teens, the **Canadian Museum of Immigration at Pier 21** offers one of Halifax's most powerful and emotional experiences. Often called "Canada's Ellis Island," Pier 21 was the entry point for nearly **one million immigrants** arriving by ship between 1928 and 1971. The museum tells their stories through multimedia exhibits, recreated cabins, and personal artifacts.

Visitors can step inside a restored immigration hall and imagine the nervous excitement of families arriving to start new lives. Interactive stations let children trace ship routes across the Atlantic, while adults can browse the **digital family history center** to search for ancestral records. The exhibits are thoughtfully designed - ***engaging enough for kids yet profound for adults*** - and they highlight Halifax's role as the gateway to Canada's multicultural identity.

The museum's location on the waterfront means you can pair your visit with lunch or a snack nearby, then take a stroll along the boardwalk afterward to reflect on the experience.

From Forts to Forums of Culture

Halifax's museums tell a larger story than any single exhibit can capture - they reflect the city's transformation from a military outpost to a hub of creativity, learning, and culture.

When Halifax was founded in 1749, its first public institutions were **forts and naval yards**. The city's identity revolved around defense and the sea. But as peace settled and commerce grew, so too did a desire for education and self-expression. By the late 19th century, schools, libraries, and societies were replacing garrisons as the city's centers of activity.

The creation of museums like the **Maritime Museum of the Atlantic** (established in 1948) and the **Art Gallery of Nova Scotia** (founded in 1908) marked a turning point. Halifax began celebrating not just what it defended, but what it created. The city's intellectual life blossomed through its universities, artists, and innovators - an evolution that continues today in the Discovery Center's cutting-edge science exhibits and the multicultural stories told at Pier 21.

Family Tips -

- **Best Time to Visit:** Most museums are open year-round, making them excellent rainy-day options or cool retreats during summer heat.
- **Ticket Deals:** Look for combination passes or "Family Admission" discounts, which often include two adults and multiple children.
- **Rainy Day Itinerary:** Start at the Discovery Center in the morning,

have lunch nearby, and visit the Maritime Museum or Art Gallery in the afternoon.
- **Accessibility:** All major museums are fully wheelchair- and stroller-accessible.
- **Interactive Bonus:** The Discovery Center and Pier 21 frequently rotate temporary exhibits - *check online before visiting to see what's new.*
- **Food Options:** The Discovery Center and Pier 21 have small cafés; otherwise, downtown eateries like **The Wooden Monkey** and **Sea Smoke** are great family-friendly spots.

Fun Facts -

- Halifax's **Discovery Center** is one of the largest science museums in Atlantic Canada.
- The **Art Gallery of Nova Scotia** is home to more than **19,000 works of art**, including the complete Maud Lewis House.
- **Gus the Tortoise** at the Museum of Natural History turned 100 in 2022, making him one of Canada's oldest living museum animals.
- Pier 21 processed nearly **one in five Canadians** with immigrant backgrounds today.
- The **CSS Acadia** in the Maritime Museum's collection served in both **World Wars** and never left Canadian waters.

In essence, Halifax's museums mirror its journey from a fortress city to a cultural capital.
They're living classrooms, keeping the past alive while inspiring the next generation to imagine what's possible.

Parks, Trails, and the Great Outdoors

Green Spaces, Open Skies, and Family Adventures

When you think of Halifax, you might picture a bustling harbor or lively downtown streets, but the city is equally defined by its green spaces. Scattered among the historic buildings and neighborhoods are parks and trails that invite you to breathe deeply, slow your pace, and reconnect with nature - *all within minutes of the urban core.*

Halifax is a city that thrives outdoors. On any warm day, families fill the Commons with picnics and soccer games, joggers weave through Shubie Park's forested paths, and cyclists cruise past lakes that shimmer in the coastal sunlight. Whether you're seeking a quiet walk, a playground for the kids, or a full-day nature adventure, Halifax offers something for every family.

The Halifax Common – The City's Green Heart

Few parks are as woven into the daily rhythm of the city as the **Halifax Common**. Established in the 1760s, it is one of **the oldest urban parks in Canada**, originally set aside as communal grazing land for livestock. Over the centuries, it has evolved into a beloved green oasis and a true reflection of Halifax's community spirit.

Today, the Common serves as the city's playground. Families gather here for open-air concerts, kite flying, and festivals that fill the fields with laughter and music. In winter, the **Oval - *a large skating rink built for the 2011 Canada Games*** - becomes a wonderland of twinkling lights and free public skating, complete with skate rentals and hot chocolate stands.

In summer, the same area transforms into a rollerblading and biking loop. It's a safe and smooth space for kids learning to ride, while parents enjoy walking laps or relaxing on nearby benches. The park's central location, bordered by Citadel Hill and bustling residential streets, makes it the city's unofficial backyard.

Families will also find playgrounds, splash pads, and shaded picnic areas scattered throughout the Common. Pack a lunch or grab takeout from nearby Quinpool Road or Robie Street - ***both lined with casual eateries***

- and settle in for an easy afternoon outdoors.

Shubie Park – Where Nature Meets History

A short drive across the harbor in Dartmouth brings you to **Shubie Park**, one of Halifax's most scenic and historically rich outdoor spaces. This 40-acre urban forest follows the path of the **Shubenacadie Canal**, a 19th-century engineering marvel that once linked Halifax Harbor to the Bay of Fundy through a chain of lakes and rivers. Though the canal was never fully completed, remnants of its stone locks still line the park's trails, offering a tangible link to Nova Scotia's early industrial past.

Families can rent canoes or kayaks from **Shubie Canal Greenway Park**, paddling along Lake Micmac and Lake Charles. The calm waters make this an excellent beginner's spot, especially for children or new paddlers. Along the way, you'll see ducks, turtles, and sometimes even herons gliding silently through the reeds.

For those who prefer land-based adventures, the **Shubie Trail System** winds through towering pine forests and gentle lakeside terrain, with multiple access points for walkers, cyclists, and joggers. Wide gravel paths make it ideal for strollers or family bike rides. At the park's center is a large playground, picnic shelters, and a canteen that sells snacks and ice cream in the summer.

It's easy to spend a full afternoon here - a picnic by the water, a paddle under the trees, and maybe a stop at the **Fairbanks Interpretation Center**, where kids can learn about the canal's history through interactive displays and model locks.

Sir Sandford Fleming Park – The Dingle and the Arm

Across the harbor on Halifax's western shore lies **Sir Sandford Fleming Park**, another family favorite known for its mix of coastal views and local history. Donated to the city in 1908 by the engineer Sir Sandford Fleming - *who also introduced Standard Time Zones to the world* - the park stretches over 95 acres of forest and shoreline along the **Northwest Arm**.

The park's most iconic feature is **The Dingle Tower**, a stone monument built to commemorate 150 years of representative government in Nova Scotia. Kids love climbing its winding interior staircase to the top, where panoramic views reveal sailboats drifting across the Arm and the skyline of downtown Halifax in the distance.

Trails weave through the park's wooded hills and connect to small beaches and picnic areas. Families often spend hours exploring - letting children splash in the shallow coves or skip stones into the gentle waves. The park's waterfront boardwalk and small playground make it especially popular on warm afternoons.

A short drive or bike ride from downtown, Fleming Park feels like a world apart. It's a peaceful escape where nature, history, and maritime scenery blend perfectly - a reminder that even in a modern city, the wild beauty of Nova Scotia is never far away.

Urban Nature and Outdoor Living

One of Halifax's greatest charms is how easily you can move from city streets to forest trails or coastal lookouts. Locals love to boast that in Halifax, **"you're never more than fifteen minutes from the ocean** or a park."

The **Chain of Lakes Trail**, stretching from Bayers Lake to Beechville, offers a safe and scenic route for biking and walking, with smooth paths perfect for families. For a shorter city loop, the **Seaport to Point Pleasant Trail** connects the boardwalk to the southern parklands - *a great way to enjoy both urban and coastal scenery in one outing.*

For pet owners, Halifax's network of **off-leash dog parks** (including sections of Point Pleasant and the Common) offers plenty of space for four-legged family members to play freely. Many parks include water stations and shaded areas, making them easy to enjoy during the warmer months.

During summer weekends, you might stumble upon outdoor yoga sessions, impromptu concerts, or food truck gatherings in these green spaces. Halifax embraces the outdoors as an extension of its social life - parks are not just places to pass through, but places to belong.

Open-Air Events and Community Spirit

Halifax's love of open-air living truly comes alive during the warmer months. **Canada Day celebrations** in the Common, **Jazz Festival performances** by the water, and **family movie nights** projected on park lawns all contribute to a lively, inclusive atmosphere.

The Halifax Common often hosts large-scale events like **Natal Day**, **Outdoor Symphony concerts**, and community fitness classes. Over in Dartmouth, **Findlay Community Center Park** holds smaller family festivals and art fairs, while **DeWolf Park in Bedford** is known for its scenic waterfront path and weekend farmers' markets.

Even in autumn and winter, the city's outdoor culture doesn't fade. Families head out to enjoy fall foliage along the **Salt Marsh Trail**, or strap on skates at the **Oval**, wrapped in scarves and the sound of local radio playing festive tunes. Halifax residents truly embrace the seasons - *and visitors quickly catch on.*

From Grazing Land to Green Haven

The story of Halifax's parks mirrors the story of the city itself - *one of transformation and community.* When the city was founded in 1749, open space was not about recreation but survival. The **Halifax Common**, established soon after settlement, was designated as a shared pasture where residents could graze cattle and store firewood. It was a utilitarian necessity, not yet the vibrant gathering place it would become.

As Halifax grew and industrialized in the 19th century, green space became a rare commodity. The Common and other emerging parks began serving a new purpose - *as lungs for the city.* By the late 1800s, urban planners recognized the need for open recreation areas, playgrounds, and tree-lined boulevards.

The introduction of **Sir Sandford Fleming Park** in the early 20th century and the preservation of **Shubie Park** later on reflected a growing environmental awareness. People began to see parks not just as land left over, but as land worth protecting - *essential to health, happiness, and community identity.*

Family Tips -

- **Best Picnic Spots:** Halifax Common (near the Oval), Dingle Park beach, or Shubie Park's lakefront shelters.
- **Getting Around:** Most parks are within a 10–15 minute drive of downtown; Shubie and Fleming have free parking.
- **Bike Rentals:** Available seasonally near the waterfront and at some park kiosks.
- **Rainy Day Alternative:** Visit the Discovery Center or Halifax Central Library's kids' floor.
- **Pet Friendly:** Many trails allow leashed dogs; Point Pleasant and sections of the Common are off-leash zones.
- **Accessibility:** Major parks like the Common and Shubie have paved or packed gravel paths suitable for strollers.

Fun Facts -

- The **Halifax Common**, dating to 1763, is one of the **oldest public parks in Canada**.
- **Shubie Park** follows the route of the **Shubenacadie Canal**, begun in 1826 to link Halifax Harbor with the Bay of Fundy.
- **Sir Sandford Fleming**, who donated his namesake park, also **invented the concept of Standard Time Zones**.
- The **Halifax Oval** is open year-round for skating in winter and rollerblading in summer - free of charge.
- Halifax's combined park system covers **more than 900 hectares** of green space.

Today, the legacy of those early visionaries lives on. Halifax's parks continue to evolve, balancing heritage with recreation and sustainability. What began as common ground for livestock has become shared ground for people - a space where the city breathes, connects, and celebrates together.

Coastal Drives and Day Trips

The coast that built a province — from fishing hamlets to icons of maritime culture.

Few regions in Canada offer as much scenic diversity within an hour's drive as Halifax. The city's coastal routes lead travelers from bustling harbors to rugged headlands, from quiet fishing coves to surfing beaches. These day trips showcase what makes Nova Scotia truly "Canada's Ocean Playground": the unbreakable bond between land, sea, and community.

Peggy's Cove – Lighthouse and Legacy

No visit to Halifax is complete without a journey to **Peggy's Cove**, the province's most famous seaside village and one of the most photographed places in the country. Only about 45 minutes southwest of downtown, the drive itself is an adventure - winding through granite outcrops, tiny fishing communities, and forested stretches that suddenly open to vast ocean views.

The star attraction, of course, is the **Peggy's Point Lighthouse**. Perched atop smooth, glacier-carved rocks, it has stood since 1915 as a sentinel over the Atlantic. Families often gather here for the view, the fresh sea breeze, and the photos that inevitably end up framed on mantels for years to come. It's a perfect place for kids to explore tidal pools and watch fishing boats return to the cove, though parents should take care near the slippery black rocks closer to the water - *signs remind visitors to stay safely back from the waves that can surge suddenly.*

Beyond the lighthouse, the **village of Peggy's Cove** offers a window into Nova Scotia's fishing heritage. Wooden wharves, lobster traps, and boats painted in sun-faded colors form a scene that feels like a living postcard. Stop by local craft shops for hand-knit sweaters, seaglass jewelry, or prints by local artists capturing the village in every light imaginable. The **Sou'Wester Restaurant**, located right beside the lighthouse, is a longtime family favorite for hot chowder and fresh fish and chips.

For a meaningful moment, many travelers also stop at the **Swissair Flight 111 Memorial**, located a few minutes away near Whalesback. This quiet granite monument honors the 229 lives lost in the 1998 plane crash just off the coast. It's a sobering reminder of the sea's power and the community's compassion - *locals were among the first to respond and comfort grieving families.*

Family Tip: *Visit Peggy's Cove in the morning or late afternoon to avoid peak crowds. Kids often enjoy drawing or painting the lighthouse from the picnic tables nearby - bring sketchbooks or disposable cameras to make it a creative memory.*

Prospect Bay and Terence Bay – Stories of the Sea

Continue your coastal adventure westward to **Prospect Bay** and **Terence Bay**, two neighboring communities that blend breathtaking scenery with poignant history. While less crowded than Peggy's Cove, they offer just as much character, and their rocky shorelines tell stories spanning centuries.

Prospect Bay is a photographer's dream, quiet harbors dotted with lobster boats, tiny islands rising offshore, and hiking trails that lead to rugged viewpoints. The **High Head Trail** is a hidden gem here: an easy-to-moderate coastal hike offering sweeping ocean vistas and picnic-perfect lookouts. Kids love spotting seabirds and, in summer, the occasional seal bobbing offshore.

Just down the road lies **Terence Bay**, a community forever linked to both triumph and tragedy. In 1873, when the **SS Atlantic** ran aground near here, more than 560 passengers lost their lives - the worst marine disaster to occur off Canada's coast before the Titanic. The people of Terence Bay risked their own safety to save others, pulling survivors from icy water and caring for them in their homes. A small **interpretive site and memorial**, along with the restored **SS Atlantic Heritage Park**, share their incredible story. The site also offers a peaceful walking path, a small beach, and picnic tables overlooking the same ocean that claimed the ship more than a century ago.

Interestingly, Terence Bay later played a role in the **Titanic connection**, too. Many of the crew members who helped recover victims after the 1912 disaster hailed from coastal Nova Scotia, and the ship that brought many bodies back to Halifax departed from these very waters. This stretch of shoreline, though calm today, has witnessed moments of both devastation and heroism that shaped maritime history.

Family Tip: *For kids fascinated by shipwrecks, combine a visit to Terence Bay with a stop at the* **Maritime Museum of the Atlantic** *back in Halifax later in your trip. There, they can see Titanic artifacts and photographs that tie together the stories of the sea.*

Lawrencetown Beach – Surf, Sand, and Salt Air

If your family craves sand between their toes and a day filled with sunshine and waves, head east from Halifax toward **Lawrencetown Beach**. About 30 minutes away via the **Marine Drive**, this stunning coastal park is beloved by surfers and beach-goers alike.

Lawrencetown is famous for its **consistent surf** - some of the best in Atlantic Canada. Even beginners can enjoy lessons at one of the local surf schools, such as the **East Coast Surf School**, which provides family-friendly instruction and gear rentals. Watching surfers ride rolling waves under a blue sky is an experience in itself, and kids often find endless entertainment collecting shells, flying kites, or chasing the foam at the water's edge.

For those who prefer a quieter scene, nearby **Conrad's Beach** and **Rainbow Haven Beach** offer gentle surf and long sandy stretches ideal for picnics and sandcastle building. Walking trails weave through dunes and salt marshes, where interpretive signs explain the delicate ecosystems and migratory bird-life.

Pack a picnic or stop at **Lawrencetown Beach Café** for smoothies and sandwiches before heading back. The coastal drive itself - *past small fishing hamlets, roadside markets, and scenic lookouts* - is as memorable as the destination.

Family Tip: Bring layers, even in summer. The ocean breeze can turn cool quickly, and the water stays chilly year-round. Don't forget sunscreen - the Atlantic wind can be deceiving on bright days.

Fisherman's Cove – A Step Back in Time

On the opposite side of Halifax Harbor, **Fisherman's Cove** in **Eastern Passage** offers an easy, relaxing day trip perfect for families. This restored 200-year-old fishing village blends old-world charm with a touch of whimsy, featuring colorful clapboard shops, local artisans, and seaside boardwalks that feel like a movie set come to life.

Stroll along the **MacCormack's Beach Provincial Park Boardwalk**, where you can watch fishing boats come and go or simply enjoy the sound of waves rolling against the rocks. Children will love spotting seabirds and browsing the souvenir shops filled with seashell crafts and maritime trinkets. The **Boondocks Restaurant** is a reliable stop for hearty seafood dishes, while the nearby **Cow's Ice Cream** stand offers a sweet finish.

Fisherman's Cove also serves as a departure point for **McNabs Island**, a natural park preserve just a short boat ride away. Families looking for a bit of adventure can pack a picnic, hop on the water taxi, and spend a few hours exploring the island's **old military fortifications, beaches, and walking trails**. It's a quieter, more natural side of Halifax that blends history, wildlife, and imagination all in one.

Family Tip: *Visit in the late afternoon when the light softens over the harbor - perfect for family photos along the boardwalk. During summer weekends, local musicians often perform live, adding to the festive coastal atmosphere.*

Making the Most of the Drive

Part of the joy of exploring Halifax's coastal routes is the journey itself. Roads like the **Lighthouse Route (Route 333)** and **Marine Drive** invite you to slow down and stop often. Roadside produce stands, galleries, and mom-and-pop restaurants dot the routes, each offering a glimpse into local life.

Keep an eye out for:

- **Tiny wharves** where fishermen sell fresh lobster right from the dock.

- **Community markets** with homemade jams and hand-knitted crafts.
- **Scenic lookouts** ideal for family photos or a few quiet minutes of ocean-gazing.

Whether you're visiting for an afternoon or a full day, each turn reveals something distinct - Nova Scotia's charm lies as much in its small moments as its big landmarks.

The Coast That Built a Province

For centuries, the coastline around Halifax has been the province's lifeline. Long before paved roads and tour buses, the sea was the highway that connected communities. Fishing villages like Peggy's Cove, Prospect, and Eastern Passage began as tiny outposts for settlers who relied on cod, mackerel, and lobster to survive. Their catch didn't just feed local families - it fueled trade with Europe and built the economic foundations of early Nova Scotia.

The same waters that sustained life also brought tragedy and change. From the shipwrecks of the 1800s to the Halifax Explosion of 1917, the ocean has tested Nova Scotians' resilience. Yet every storm, every loss, seemed to strengthen the coastal bond - *people rebuilt, shared, and kept faith in the sea's promise.*

Today, the lighthouses that dot these shores serve as more than navigational aids. They are symbols of endurance and hope, guiding not just ships but the spirit of a province.

Fun Facts -

- The **Peggy's Cove Lighthouse** is one of the most photographed landmarks in all of Canada.
- **Lawrencetown Beach** hosts international surf competitions and attracts surfers from around the world year-round.
- The **Halifax–Dartmouth ferry** connects travelers to many of these day-trip routes via easy public transport links.
- **McNabs Island**, visible from Fisherman's Cove, once housed over 1,000 residents, military barracks, and a Victorian picnic ground.
- The **Lighthouse Route (Route 333)** is part of Nova Scotia's scenic travel system, known for its handcrafted signage and ocean-view turnouts.

For visitors, following this coastline is more than a scenic drive - it's a journey through the stories that shaped Atlantic Canada's soul.

Food, Flavor, and Family Dining

From seaport sustenance to culinary capital - how Halifax's food culture grew from the docks up.

For a city shaped by the sea, Halifax has always had a close relationship with food. What began as a necessity for sailors, settlers, and fishermen has evolved into a vibrant culinary culture that celebrates local ingredients, family traditions, and global influences. Today, Halifax's dining scene balances old-fashioned comfort with fresh creativity, making it one of Atlantic Canada's most exciting - *and family-friendly* - places to eat.

From crispy fish and chips by the harbor to warm donairs dripping with sweet sauce, there's something for every appetite here. Families can snack their way from waterfront patios to farmers' markets, stopping for ice cream cones, blueberry desserts, and maybe a taste of lobster along the way.

Let's dive in - fork first!

Seaside Classics: Fish, Chips, and Lobster Rolls

If Halifax had a signature flavor, it would be the taste of the ocean - *salty, simple, and satisfying*. For generations, locals have relied on the bounty of the Atlantic, and seafood remains the city's most beloved culinary cornerstone.

Fish and chips are a must-try for families, available from dozens of cozy restaurants and takeout shacks across the city. The crispy batter, flaky haddock, and golden fries are comfort food at its finest. Try **The Battery Park Beer Bar** in Dartmouth for a modern twist, or **The Five Fishermen Grill** downtown for a sit-down version that nods to

Halifax's maritime heritage. On sunny days, few things beat the casual charm of **The Fry Daddy's** or **The Waterfront Warehouse**, where kids can eat with a view of the boats drifting past.

Then there's the **lobster roll** - *a summer icon*. Traditionally served on a buttered, toasted bun with just enough mayo to bind the tender chunks of lobster, it's a staple at seaside eateries like **The Bicycle Thief**, **Salty's**, or **Evan's Seafood**. Some spots get creative, adding lemon zest or herbs, but the best rolls let the lobster shine. Pair one with local root beer or a craft soda for the perfect Halifax picnic.

Families visiting in late spring or summer might even catch a **lobster supper** at a community hall or church in nearby coastal villages. These events - *complete with chowder, mussels, and homemade pie* - are part meal, part Maritime tradition, offering a warm welcome to visitors and locals alike.

Family Tip: *Many waterfront restaurants open earlier in the day to cater to cruise ship passengers. Arriving for an early lunch means smaller crowds, faster service, and better seating with a view.*

Halifax's Iconic Donair: A Sweet and Savoury Legend

If Halifax has a food with cult status, it's the **donair** - *the city's official dish since 2015*.

It began in the 1970s when a Greek immigrant, Peter Gamoulakos, adapted the traditional gyro for local tastes at his King of Donair restaurant on Quinpool Road. Instead of lamb and tzatziki, he used spiced beef and a sweet, garlicky sauce made with condensed milk, vinegar, and sugar - *an unexpected but irresistible combination*.

Today, the Halifax donair is a rite of passage for visitors and a late-night classic for locals. Families can sample milder versions earlier in the day at spots like **Johnny K's Authentic Donair** or **Tony's Famous Donair**, where generous portions and friendly service keep the tradition alive. Even kids often enjoy donair poutine - *fries topped with donair meat, cheese, and sauce* - a fun, shareable twist on a local icon.

You'll spot donair pizzas, donair egg rolls, even donair-flavoured chips across Nova Scotia. What began as a single restaurant experiment has become a full-blown part of the province's identity.

Family Tip: *If your kids prefer less spice, ask for "light sauce" or a half portion. Many donair shops now offer smaller, family-size servings or even "build-your-own" options for picky eaters.*

Halifax Seaport Farmers' Market – A Taste of Local Life

Located near the cruise terminal and waterfront boardwalk, the **Halifax Seaport Farmers' Market** is more than a place to shop - it's a feast for the senses and a celebration of Nova Scotia's agricultural roots. Founded in 1750, it's one of the oldest continuously operating markets in North America.

Families can wander from stall to stall sampling fresh baked goods, local cheeses, smoked fish, and seasonal fruits. Kids are drawn to the colorful produce stands and the scent of maple-glazed nuts or warm pastries.

There's plenty of space to sit, snack, and people-watch, and local artisans often sell handcrafted souvenirs that make thoughtful mementos of your visit. Don't miss the **Blueberry Pancake stall** on weekend mornings or the **Acadian Kitchen** stand, where you can try traditional dishes like rappie pie or fricot stew.

During summer, live music fills the air outside the market, and families can relax on the nearby **Harbourwalk** lawn with picnic blankets. It's one of the easiest places in the city to experience Halifax's spirit - *friendly, open, and full of flavor.*

Family Tip: *Arrive early on Saturdays for the best selection, especially during blueberry or strawberry season. Parking fills up quickly, but the walk from downtown is short and scenic.*

Family-Friendly Breweries and Waterfront Patios

Halifax's craft beer scene has exploded over the past decade, but what sets it apart is how inclusive it is for families. Many breweries double as community gathering spots with outdoor patios, kid-friendly menus, and games for all ages.

Garrison Brewing near the Seaport Market offers picnic tables and ocean breezes, while **Propeller Brewing** on Gottingen Street provides root beer and craft sodas made in-house for younger visitors. Over in Dartmouth, **Brightwood Brewery** pairs local beer with food trucks and family seating, making it a great spot after exploring Alderney Landing.

For families who prefer waterfront dining, restaurants like **The Bicycle Thief** and **Stubborn Goat Beer Garden** combine excellent views with relaxed service. Parents can enjoy a local pint while kids dig into flatbreads, pasta, or fish tacos. On summer evenings, street performers and live bands along the boardwalk keep everyone entertained.

Family Tip: *Many Halifax breweries host Sunday brunches with pancakes, breakfast sandwiches, and live acoustic music - an easygoing way to experience local life together.*

Sweet Treats and Ice Cream Trails

After a day exploring Halifax, few things delight kids (and adults) more than ice cream. Fortunately, the city has an abundance of options, from nostalgic parlors to trendy artisan spots.

COWS Ice Cream, with its playful cow-themed decor, is a must-visit on the waterfront. Originating in Prince Edward Island, it's known for creamy, locally made flavors like Moo Henry and Wowie Cowie. Over in the North End, **Dee Dee's Ice Cream** serves handmade scoops using organic ingredients and Nova Scotia fruit - *their blueberry flavor is legendary.*

Halifax is also part of Nova Scotia's **Ice Cream Trail**, which connects parlors across the province. Families can "collect" stops, trying different flavors as they travel, from Mahone Bay to the Annapolis Valley.

Beyond ice cream, Halifax offers plenty of other sweet indulgences. Try **Sugar Bakery** for cupcakes and cookies, **Two If By Sea** for massive croissants, or **The Old Apothecary** for artisanal pastries served in a cozy setting.

Family Tip: *Many ice cream spots along the boardwalk stay open late in summer - perfect for an evening stroll after dinner with harbor lights reflecting on the water.*

Blueberry Bliss: Nova Scotia's Favorite Dessert Fruit

Nova Scotia's wild blueberries deserve their own spotlight. The province is one of the world's top producers, and Halifax celebrates them in every possible form - *pies, tarts, jams, pancakes, and smoothies.*

Late summer is **blueberry season**, and families can find them at roadside stands or pick-your-own farms within an hour's drive of the city. Restaurants highlight them in desserts and cocktails, while bakeries roll out limited-time blueberry specials.

For a true local experience, visit **The Middle Spoon Desserterie** downtown, where the blueberry crumble and lemon tart are local favorites. Or head to the **Seaport Farmers' Market** for jars of wild blueberry jam to take home - *a sweet souvenir that tastes like summer in Nova Scotia.*

From Seaport Sustenance to Culinary Capital

Halifax's relationship with food began long before it became a tourist destination. When the city was founded in 1749, it served as a British naval stronghold and supply hub. Sailors and settlers relied on the port's access to the sea and surrounding farmland for survival. Salted cod, hardtack, and rum were staples - far from gourmet, but vital for endurance.

As trade expanded through the 18th and 19th centuries, Halifax's harbor became a crossroads of cultures and cuisines. The city welcomed waves of immigrants - ***Acadian, Scottish, Irish, African Nova Scotian, and more*** - each bringing their own flavors, techniques, and traditions. These influences slowly transformed local food from survival fare to celebration.

By the 20th century, Halifax's dining scene reflected both its working-class roots and its growing cosmopolitan flair. The dockside diners that once fed sailors evolved into neighborhood restaurants serving chowder and fishcakes, while postwar prosperity introduced family-run bakeries, coffee houses, and pubs. The arrival of international students and newcomers added even more diversity - today you can find authentic Lebanese shawarma, Korean barbecue, and Indian curries just blocks from traditional seafood shacks.

What makes Halifax special is that its culinary story is still unfolding. The same harbor that once supplied salt cod to the British Navy now welcomes cruise ships and food festivals. The same markets that once sold survival rations now overflow with farm-fresh produce and artisanal cheese.

Fun Facts -

- The **"Halifax Donair"** was officially declared the city's signature food in 2015.
- The **Halifax Seaport Farmers' Market**, founded in 1750, is one of North America's oldest.
- **Nova Scotia wild blueberries** are smaller and sweeter than cultivated ones, growing naturally in glacial soil.
- The province's **Ice Cream Trail** includes over 60 stops each summer.
- Many **Halifax breweries** produce craft sodas and root beer for kids alongside their traditional brews.

FOOD, FLAVOR, AND FAMILY DINING

*Through it all, the spirit remains the same: good food, shared with good company,
in a place where the ocean is never far away.*

Arts, Culture, and Local Spirit

Halifax isn't just a harbor city; it's a stage. Every street corner hums with creativity - from painted murals and fiddle tunes to theatrical performances and open-air festivals that transform the downtown core into a cultural carnival. Whether you're visiting as a family, couple, or group of curious travelers, the city's artistic spirit is impossible to miss.

ARTS, CULTURE, AND LOCAL SPIRIT

Neptune Theater – Stories That Come Alive

At the heart of downtown Halifax, on Argyle Street, stands **Neptune Theater**, a cornerstone of the city's performing arts scene and one of the oldest professional theaters in Canada. Since opening its doors in 1963, Neptune has welcomed generations of performers and audiences alike. Today, it offers two stages - the main Fountain Hall for large productions and the smaller Scotiabank Stage for more intimate performances.

Families will find something for everyone here: from **classic musicals like** *The Sound of Music* to **original plays featuring Atlantic stories and humor**. The theater's annual holiday production - *often a playful twist on fairy tales like Cinderella or Peter Pan* - has become a beloved tradition for locals and visitors.

For families traveling with children, Neptune also runs **youth workshops and summer camps**, helping kids build confidence while exploring the art of performance. Parents can enjoy a relaxed evening show knowing their little ones have spent the day learning stagecraft in a nurturing environment.

Family Tip: *Seats toward the back of Fountain Hall's main floor provide a great view for younger kids who might find the balcony too high.*

The Art Gallery of Nova Scotia – A Maritime Masterpiece

Just steps from the waterfront, the **Art Gallery of Nova Scotia (AGNS)** is where creativity meets coastal identity. Home to more than **19,000 works**, it's Atlantic Canada's largest art museum and a fascinating place for families to experience the region's imagination through painting, sculpture, photography, and folk art.

One of the gallery's most famous collections is dedicated to **Maud Lewis**, the self-taught folk artist whose brightly colored depictions of Nova Scotia's rural life have captivated the world. Children often delight in seeing Maud's **tiny restored house**, complete with its cheerful, hand-painted furniture and walls - *a space so small yet so filled with joy that it embodies the spirit of resilience and simplicity.*

Beyond its exhibits, AGNS often hosts **hands-on family days**, where children can make art inspired by what they see. The staff provide gentle guidance and encourage creativity, making it a relaxed way to introduce kids to art appreciation.

Family Tip: *The museum café offers kid-friendly options and makes a great stop before or after exploring the nearby Halifax waterfront.*

Street Art and Public Murals – Halifax as an Open-Air Gallery

Art in Halifax doesn't stay behind museum walls - *it spills out into the streets.* The city's murals and graffiti are stories painted in color, from the side of old warehouses to the underpasses near Gottingen Street and the North End.

The **Halifax Mural Festival**, launched in 2022, has added an explosion of vibrancy to urban spaces, showcasing both local and international artists. Families can take a **self-guided mural walk**, discovering pieces that reflect community pride, social messages, or maritime imagery.

Among the most photographed murals are:

- The **"Welcome to Halifax"** mural at the ferry terminal - a bright

and bold greeting for visitors.
- The **Seahorse Tavern mural**, celebrating Halifax's music legacy.
- Colorful depictions of marine life around the waterfront boardwalk that double as great selfie spots.

It's a free and fun way for kids to engage with art without the quiet rules of a gallery - *perfect for stroller-friendly sightseeing.*

Family Tip: *Combine your mural hunt with a stop for gelato at Humani-T Café on South Park Street or coffee for the adults while the kids enjoy smoothies.*

Local Musicians – The Soundtrack of the City

Music is as much a part of Halifax as the sea breeze. From buskers on the boardwalk to pub sessions spilling out onto Argyle Street patios, the city lives to a maritime rhythm.

The **Busker Festival**, held every August along the waterfront, transforms the city into a global stage where performers from every corner of the world entertain families with acrobatics, juggling, and musical talent. Kids are especially captivated by the energy and humor - *it's impossible not to smile.*

Beyond the festivals, Halifax's local music scene thrives year-round.

- The **Carleton Music Bar & Grill** offers all-ages matinee shows on weekends.
- The **Seahorse Tavern** and **The Local** host live Celtic or folk nights, often free to attend before evening hours.

- During summer, **Public Gardens and Grand Parade Square** frequently feature outdoor concerts - *perfect for a picnic and dance in the grass.*

From traditional fiddle tunes to indie rock, Halifax's musical heartbeat never slows.

Family Tip: *Check the Halifax Events Calendar or Discover Halifax website before your trip - many local performances are free and ideal for kids.*

Festivals That Bring Halifax to Life

Halifax Jazz Festival

Held every July, the **Halifax Jazz Festival** (or "Jazz-fest") transforms the waterfront and downtown venues into a week-long celebration of sound. What began in 1987 as a modest gathering now welcomes **more than 65,000 visitors** each year. The family-friendly **main stage tent** near the waterfront features international jazz artists, while free daytime performances take place in public squares and libraries.

Families can attend workshops, rhythm circles, and dance lessons that encourage everyone - ***even toddlers*** - to move to the beat.

Busker Festival

Since its first edition in **1986**, the **Halifax International Busker Festival** has become one of the city's most anticipated summer events. Performers from as far as Australia, Japan, and the UK take over the waterfront for over a week of laughter and spectacle. Children are often chosen as volunteers during shows, adding to the excitement.

Don't forget small change - though the performances are free, buskers rely on audience tips.

Holiday and Cultural Festivals
Come December, Halifax glows with winter charm.

- The **Evergreen Festival** combines Christmas markets, light displays, and outdoor performances along the waterfront.
- Families can enjoy **carolers at Historic Properties**, hot chocolate stands, and skating at the Emera Oval.

Year-round, Halifax also celebrates multicultural events like **Greek Fest**, **African Heritage Month**, and **Natal Day** - a civic celebration marking the founding of Halifax in 1749. Each event invites visitors to experience a piece of the city's identity through dance, food, and community spirit.

Rainy Day Arts and Culture for Families

Halifax's coastal weather can be unpredictable, but rainy days don't mean staying inside your hotel. The city offers several **indoor creative escapes**:

- **Discovery Center:** This hands-on science museum on Lower Water Street combines innovation and fun. Kids can explore exhibits on energy, space, and motion - often featuring art-themed installations and maker workshops.
- **The Clay Café:** A favorite among families, it lets visitors paint their own pottery pieces. Parents can relax with coffee while kids create their next masterpiece.
- **Central Library's Creative Lab:** Offers 3D printing, music recording, and design stations - *a modern twist on art and storytelling*.

These spots keep the spirit of Halifax's creativity alive, no matter the weather.

Family Dining with an Artistic Twist

After soaking up culture and sound, families can dine at **restaurants and cafés that celebrate local art and music.**

- **The Old Triangle Irish Alehouse** often features live folk bands during dinner hours, perfect for a relaxed evening.
- **The Wooden Monkey** (with locations downtown and in Dartmouth) displays work by Nova Scotia artists and serves organic, locally sourced meals - including kid-friendly favorites like mac and cheese with real cheddar.
- **Two If By Sea Café** in Dartmouth is known for its giant croissants and gallery-like vibe, often showcasing rotating art from local photographers.

For dessert, the Cows Ice Cream on the boardwalk adds a creative touch to classic maritime

Halifax's Creative Pulse

Halifax's identity as Atlantic Canada's cultural capital didn't appear overnight - *it was built through resilience and reinvention.*

In the early 19th century, Halifax was primarily a naval stronghold, with its energy focused on defense and trade. Yet even then, its multicultural character was brewing: Scottish settlers brought ceilidhs and fiddles; African Nova Scotians carried the rhythms of gospel and jazz; Mi'kmaq artisans preserved storytelling through carvings and beadwork.

ARTS, CULTURE, AND LOCAL SPIRIT

By the 20th century, the city had evolved into a **hub of expression**, its post-war population embracing education, performance, and literature. Neptune Theater's founding in the 1960s symbolized this shift - *a declaration that Halifax was not just a port but a place of imagination.*

Street music, student artists, and maritime crafts all wove together to create a **community that celebrates creativity as survival**. The city's artists didn't wait for opportunity; they built it themselves, often turning empty spaces and old buildings into studios and performance halls.

Fun Facts -

- The **Halifax Busker Festival** is the longest-running of its kind in North America.
- **Neptune Theater** once hosted a surprise appearance by *Anne Murray*, one of Nova Scotia's most famous musical exports.
- The **Art Gallery of Nova Scotia**'s Maud Lewis house is so small that the entire structure could fit into one modern living room.
- Halifax's **public pianos** - *scattered across downtown* - invite anyone to sit down and play a tune.

Family Tips -

- Many Halifax festivals are **free to attend**, but parking can be limited - *consider walking or using public transit.*
- For **quiet moments between shows**, the Halifax Public Gardens or waterfront benches are ideal for snack breaks.
- Bring a **sketchbook or small journal** - children often love drawing the murals or performances they've seen, creating a personal art souvenir from the trip.

Today, Halifax's art scene reflects the same qualities that define its people: resilient, authentic, and welcoming. Creativity here isn't a luxury - it's part of life. It spills from stages to sidewalks, reminding visitors that Halifax's heart beats to the rhythm of community spirit and coastal inspiration.

History in Every Corner

Halifax's skyline may be modern and lively, but beneath every clock tower, cobblestone, and church steeple lies a chapter of a story centuries in the making. The city's past isn't confined to museums - it lingers in its architecture, its harbor, and even in the quiet corners of old cemeteries where history whispers among the trees.

For families exploring Halifax, history here feels alive. From the steadfast hands of the **Old Town Clock** to the solemn grounds of the **Titanic graves**, every landmark reveals how this harbor city became one of Canada's most storied destinations.

St. Paul's Church – The Oldest Building in Halifax

Standing proudly on Argyle Street since **1750, St. Paul's Anglican Church** is not only the oldest building in Halifax but also the oldest Protestant church in Canada. Its Georgian design and white clapboard exterior make it instantly recognizable amid the bustle of downtown. Yet behind its graceful simplicity lies a wealth of stories.

Built just one year after Halifax was founded, St. Paul's has witnessed the city's triumphs and tragedies alike - from royal visits to fires, storms, and explosions. Step inside and the past greets you immediately: polished wooden pews, historic plaques, and sunlight filtering through windows that have seen nearly three centuries of change.

One of the church's most mysterious features captures the imagination of visitors - **a silhouette embedded in one of its windows**, said to have appeared during the **1917 Halifax Explosion**. The shape resembles the profile of a man, and though experts have debated the cause for decades, the legend endures that it's the image of a parishioner caught in the blast's shock-wave.

Guided tours are available during summer months, and the church's caretakers are welcoming to visitors with children. Kids often enjoy searching for details - from the Royal Coat of Arms to the original 18th-century pews once reserved for military officers.

Family Tip: *The churchyard is shaded and peaceful, making it a good rest stop during a downtown walking day. Parents can enjoy a quiet moment while kids stretch their legs.*

HISTORY IN EVERY CORNER

The Old Town Clock – Halifax's Timeless Landmark

Perched on the slope of Citadel Hill and gazing down over Brunswick Street, the **Old Town Clock** is one of Halifax's most beloved symbols. Installed in **1803** by order of **Prince Edward, Duke of Kent**, the clock was meant to bring punctuality to the garrison stationed at the Halifax Citadel. Over two centuries later, it's still ticking - *a steadfast guardian of the city's rhythm*.

Its elegant three-tiered design, topped with a green copper dome, makes it both a landmark and a reminder of Halifax's military roots. The clock's mechanism, crafted by the House of Vulliamy in London, remains an intricate masterpiece of engineering.

Families visiting the area can combine a trip to the clock with a **walk up Citadel Hill**, where sweeping views of downtown and the harbor await. In summer, costumed guides and re-enactors march in full regimental dress, giving kids a vivid sense of Halifax's 19th-century past.

If you time your visit right, you'll hear the **noon cannon**, fired daily from the fortress - a tradition that has continued almost uninterrupted since **1857**.

Family Tip: *Bring binoculars or a camera zoom lens - kids love spotting the clock's face from different parts of the city, turning it into a "find the clock" challenge as they explore.*

Province House – The Birthplace of Responsible Government

On the corner of Hollis and George Streets stands **Province House**, a masterpiece of Palladian architecture and the home of Nova Scotia's legislature since **1819**. It's often overlooked by casual visitors, but this modest sandstone building has a claim to fame that shaped Canadian democracy.

In **1848**, Nova Scotia became the first colony in the British Empire to achieve **responsible government** - meaning the executive branch was accountable to the elected assembly rather than to the Crown's appointed representatives. It was a quiet revolution that would later influence political reform across Canada.

Today, visitors can take free guided tours of Province House (when the legislature is not in session). Inside, the **Red Chamber** and **Legislative Library** display portraits, historic documents, and finely preserved architecture. The staff are accustomed to welcoming families, and guides often tailor their stories for young visitors - *highlighting how decisions made here helped shape modern Canada.*

Outside, the **grounds feature interpretive panels** explaining Nova Scotia's political milestones. It's an easy stop between the waterfront and Spring Garden Road, ideal for a quick educational visit before lunch.

Family Tip: *Encourage kids to imagine they're members of the early Assembly debating how to build a new province - it's a great way to spark interest in Canadian history.*

Fairview Lawn Cemetery – The Titanic Connection

On a quiet hill in the city's North End lies one of Halifax's most visited historic sites: **Fairview Lawn Cemetery**. While many cemeteries hold local heroes, this one holds global tragedy - *it is the final resting place of 121 victims of the Titanic disaster.*

After the RMS *Titanic* sank in April 1912, Halifax became a recovery center for the North Atlantic, as ships from the city were dispatched to retrieve bodies from the icy waters. The victims who could not be identified or claimed were laid to rest here.

Rows of simple grey granite headstones, arranged in a gentle curve resembling the bow of a ship, mark the graves. Among them lies the marker for the **"Unknown Child"**, long a symbol of the human heartbreak behind the legend. DNA testing in 2007 finally confirmed his identity as **Sidney Leslie Goodwin,** a 19-month-old English boy traveling with his family. Visitors often leave flowers or small toys by his grave, moved by the enduring story.

Another grave, that of **J. Dawson,** attracts attention due to its connection with Leonardo DiCaprio's fictional character from *Titanic*, though the real Dawson was a crewman from Ireland.

Families visiting the site find it to be a peaceful, reflective experience. Interpretive signs explain the city's role in the tragedy and provide context for younger visitors.

Family Tip: *The cemetery paths are hilly but well-kept - wear comfortable shoes and bring water. For children, discuss the story beforehand so they understand the memorial's solemn nature.*

Halifax Explosion Memorials – Remembering 1917

No single event shaped Halifax's identity more profoundly than the **Halifax Explosion of December 6, 1917.** When the munitions ship *Mont-Blanc* collided with the *Imo* in the harbor, the resulting blast - *the largest human-made explosion before the atomic age* - obliterated much of the city's North End, killing nearly 2,000 people and injuring thousands more.

Today, the legacy of that morning lives on in several **memorials and interpretive trails** throughout Halifax.

Fort Needham Memorial Park

The most significant site is **Fort Needham Memorial Park**, located near the heart of the explosion's impact zone. The **Halifax Explosion Memorial Bell Tower**, standing tall among trees and open lawns, offers sweeping views of the harbor and a place for quiet reflection. Each year on December 6th, the community gathers here for a ceremony of remembrance.

Families can walk the **interpretive trail** that winds through the park, reading panels that recount survivors' stories and how neighbors rebuilt their lives from the ruins. It's a moving experience, yet one that emphasizes resilience and unity over despair.

Hydrostone District

Just a short walk from Fort Needham lies the **Hydrostone neighborhood**, a testament to recovery and renewal. After the explosion, this area was rebuilt using "hydrostone," a type of concrete block designed for fire resistance and stability. The result was one of North America's earliest planned communities - *complete with green spaces and tree-lined* *boulevards.*

Today, Hydrostone Market is a vibrant hub of cafés, bakeries, and boutiques - *a perfect stop for lunch after visiting the memorial.* Kids can enjoy treats from **Julien's Bakery** or **Epicurious Morsels**, while parents browse local art and handmade crafts.

Anchoring History: The Explosion Bell

Inside the **Maritime Museum of the Atlantic**, visitors can find another poignant artifact - the **Explosion Bell**, rung each year to honor those lost. It's one of Halifax's most sacred traditions, and for many, it symbolizes how the city carries its past with quiet dignity.

Family Tip: *Start your visit at the museum for context, then head to Fort Needham and Hydrostone for an on-site experience of remembrance and rebuilding.*

Walking Through Time – Connecting the Landmarks

What makes Halifax special is how its history connects across short distances. Families can easily turn this chapter's landmarks into a **half-day walking itinerary**:

1. Begin at **Citadel Hill** to view the Old Town Clock.
2. Walk down to **St. Paul's Church** and nearby **Province House** for a taste of 18th- and 19th-century life.
3. Continue north by bus or car to **Fairview Lawn Cemetery** to reflect on the Titanic's story.
4. End at **Fort Needham Memorial Park** and the **Hydrostone Market** for lunch and learning.

Each stop adds a layer to the story of Halifax - *from colonial roots to global connections and the strength born from tragedy.*

Tragedy and Triumph

The soul of Halifax is shaped by its resilience. Few cities in the world have endured and rebuilt as this one has.

The **Halifax Explosion** was not merely a local catastrophe - *it was a moment that tested the very spirit of Canada.* Entire neighborhoods vanished in an instant, yet within hours, survivors began rescuing one another. Relief poured in from across the country and even from **Boston**, whose swift aid created a bond that endures to this day. *(Each year, Nova Scotia sends Boston a* **Christmas tree** *as a token of gratitude - a gesture that has become a beloved international tradition.)*

The rebuilding effort gave Halifax new life: safer housing, improved planning, and a deeper appreciation for community. From the ashes of 1917, a city emerged that valued cooperation over isolation and compassion over complacency.

In that sense, every site - *from the Old Town Clock's steady rhythm to the calm of Fairview Lawn Cemetery* - tells a piece of the same story: **Halifax endures.**

Fun Facts -

- The **Old Town Clock** has been ticking continuously for over **220 years**, maintained by Parks Canada.
- **St. Paul's Church** once served as a makeshift hospital after the Halifax Explosion.

- The **Hydrostone District** is one of Canada's first examples of urban renewal and remains a designated heritage area.
- Halifax's annual **Christmas tree gift to Boston** began in 1918 and continues to this day.

Family Tips -

- Many historic sites, including Province House and St. Paul's, offer **free admission**.
- The **Citadel and Old Town Clock** are stroller-accessible with nearby washrooms.
- Plan visits to outdoor memorials earlier in the day to avoid afternoon heat or wind on the hilltops.
- Use a **Halifax Transit Day Pass** for easy travel between landmarks if exploring with kids.

Through wars, storms, fires, and loss, the city's people have rebuilt again and again, carrying forward a collective memory that honors both grief and growth. That is what gives Halifax its character - not just history in every corner, but hope in every heart.

Beyond Halifax: Regional Family Excursions

The Appeal of Halifax's Surroundings

While Halifax's heart beats strongest along its bustling waterfront, much of its soul lies just beyond city limits. Within an hour's drive, families can find themselves among rolling countryside, sparkling lakes, coastal fishing villages, and fertile farmlands. These are the landscapes that shaped Nova Scotia's identity - a blend of maritime endurance, rural pride, and natural wonder.

For families exploring beyond downtown, day trips from Halifax offer more than scenery; they promise connection. Children can paddle at quiet beaches, visit working farms, or cycle on trails reclaimed from railway lines. Parents can sip coffee in small-town cafés, stroll through heritage sites, and experience the welcoming rhythm of life outside the city.

This chapter takes you through some of the most rewarding destinations just beyond Halifax - *places like Bedford, Hammonds Plains, and the Musquodoboit Valley* - before stretching farther afield to Lunenburg's seaside charm and Wolfville's orchard-filled valleys. Each destination captures a different side of Nova Scotia, yet all share one quality in common: the sense that time moves a little slower here, inviting visitors to pause, explore, and breathe in the Atlantic air.

Bedford Basin and Hammonds Plains

Only a 20-minute drive from downtown Halifax, Bedford feels like a small town folded neatly into the edge of the city. Nestled at the north end of Halifax Harbor, the Bedford Basin is both historic and picturesque — once the staging area for wartime convoys and now a peaceful haven for sailors, walkers, and families looking for an afternoon escape.

Bedford Waterfront and DeWolf Park

The Bedford Waterfront has become one of the most family-friendly promenades in the region. DeWolf Park, with its boardwalk stretching along the water's edge, offers playgrounds, picnic areas, and sweeping views of the basin where yachts and sailboats bob gently in the tide.

Parents can enjoy a coffee from a nearby café while kids race along the path, collecting seashells or counting passing boats.

In summer, the waterfront comes alive with local markets and music festivals, while spring and autumn bring quieter moments - perfect for a leisurely walk or an impromptu family photo shoot against the backdrop of calm waters and distant city skylines.

Hammonds Plains and the Call of the Lakes

Travel inland from Bedford, and the roads lead you through Hammonds Plains - a community laced with forest trails, shimmering lakes, and country charm. This area offers an ideal mix of adventure and relaxation for families who enjoy the outdoors but prefer something quieter than the coast.

The **Blue Mountain–Birch Cove Lakes Wilderness Area** is one of the hidden gems here. Trails wind through forest and granite ridges to secluded lakes, offering peaceful paddling and wildlife spotting. In autumn, the maple-lined paths blaze with color, and families can often spot loons or even a deer crossing the water's edge.

Hammonds Plains also has a growing reputation for local dining and recreation. Stop by one of its small family-run restaurants or bakeries for hearty Nova Scotia fare - seafood chowder, baked goods, and locally sourced comfort foods. For those traveling with kids, nearby indoor play centers and skating rinks make for great rainy-day options.

Musquodoboit Valley Rail Trail and Wildlife Parks

Venture east of Halifax, and you'll find yourself entering a landscape of broad valleys, old forests, and winding rivers - the Musquodoboit Valley. This is rural Nova Scotia at its best: quiet, welcoming, and full of opportunities to reconnect with nature.

The Musquodoboit Trailway

At the heart of the region lies the **Musquodoboit Trailway**, a scenic multi-use path stretching over 15 kilometers along a converted railway line. It's part of the national **Trans Canada Trail** network, linking Halifax's metropolitan area to the wild heart of the province.

Cyclists, walkers, and families with strollers will find the route gentle and rewarding. The trail passes through forests, wetlands, and river valleys, with occasional rest areas that make ideal picnic stops. Along the way, interpretive signs highlight the region's ecology and its history as a key transportation corridor during Nova Scotia's railway era.

For those seeking more adventure, side trails like the **Admiral Lake Loop** climb to scenic lookouts, revealing sweeping views of granite cliffs and deep blue lakes. Bring a packed lunch and spend the day exploring - *you'll find few better examples of the province's rugged natural beauty within such easy reach of the city.*

Wildlife and Family Adventures

Beyond the trailway, the valley offers rich encounters with local wildlife. Keep an eye out for bald eagles circling above or turtles sunning themselves along the riverbanks. Families can visit **Hope for Wildlife**, a well-known animal rehabilitation center that rescues injured or orphaned wildlife and occasionally hosts open-house events where visitors can learn about conservation efforts up close.

The Musquodoboit Valley is also home to small local museums and community fairs that celebrate rural life - *perfect for families wanting a taste of Nova Scotia's agricultural heritage.* In late summer, farm stands overflow with fresh corn, berries, and local honey, simple pleasures that make day trips here as satisfying as they are scenic.

Cole Harbor Heritage Farm

Closer to the city, **Cole Harbor Heritage Farm Museum** is one of the most beloved family attractions in the Halifax region. Located just 15 minutes from downtown, the farm offers a living glimpse into Nova Scotia's rural past.

Children can meet friendly farm animals - **sheep, chickens, pigs, and cows** - while parents stroll through heritage gardens and restored barns. The museum buildings showcase artifacts and displays on how families once lived and worked on the land, reflecting the strong agricultural traditions that supported the province for centuries.

What makes Cole Harbor special is its blend of education and relaxation. Kids can learn where their food comes from while enjoying open green spaces to run and play. The on-site café, serving homemade soups, sandwiches, and desserts, adds a comforting touch for parents looking to pause mid-day.

Throughout the year, the farm hosts seasonal festivals such as the **Spring Garden Party** and **Harvest Fair**, complete with live music, demonstrations, and traditional games. It's an ideal place for families to experience the hands-on, community-based spirit that defines Nova

Scotia's countryside.

Short Trips to Lunenburg and Wolfville

Sometimes, the best family experiences lie just a little farther afield. Within a 90-minute drive from Halifax are two destinations that consistently rank among Nova Scotia's most rewarding day or weekend trips: the colorful seaside town of **Lunenburg** and the lush Annapolis Valley's cultural hub, **Wolfville**.

Lunenburg – A Seaside Storybook

Lunenburg is a UNESCO World Heritage Site, and it feels every bit like a living postcard. Founded in 1753, the town's brightly painted waterfront buildings, narrow streets, and working harbor create a perfect blend of charm and authenticity. Families can stroll the **Lunenburg Waterfront**, where the famed **Bluenose II**, Nova Scotia's iconic schooner, often docks.

The **Fisheries Museum of the Atlantic** is a must-visit for curious kids. Its interactive exhibits - *including real fishing boats to board and touch tanks filled with local marine life* - bring the region's seafaring heritage to life. Parents will appreciate the history, while children delight in the hands-on learning.

Local restaurants serve up some of the freshest seafood in the province, from scallops to lobster rolls. For dessert, grab homemade ice cream and wander through the hilly streets, where art galleries and craft shops invite leisurely exploration.

If time allows, the drive to Lunenburg itself is a scenic highlight, passing through **Mahone Bay**, famous for its three waterfront churches and boutique shops. Families can easily make a full day of this coastal circuit - *Halifax to Mahone Bay to Lunenburg and back* - enjoying a taste of both maritime history and modern small-town creativity.

Wolfville – Orchards, Vines, and Valley Views

In contrast to the salt air of Lunenburg, **Wolfville** offers fertile farmland, vineyards, and apple orchards stretching as far as the eye can see. It's the beating heart of the Annapolis Valley, known for its food culture, farm-to-table experiences, and outdoor recreation.

Families can visit **Grand-Pré National Historic Site**, a beautifully landscaped park and interpretive center commemorating the Acadian people and their enduring cultural legacy. Kids can explore open fields, heritage gardens, and interactive exhibits, while adults appreciate the depth of Nova Scotia's French heritage.

Wolfville's **Farmers' Market** (held year-round) is a feast for the senses, filled with local produce, baked goods, and handmade crafts. For children, the friendly atmosphere and live music make it as entertaining as it is educational.

Nearby wineries like **Lightfoot & Wolfville** or **Benjamin Bridge** welcome families, offering wide lawns and picnic areas where kids can play while parents sample local wines. Autumn brings apple-picking season - *a timeless Nova Scotian tradition that blends fun, food, and family connection.*

The drive to Wolfville also passes several roadside lookouts, including the **Evangeline Beach** area, where visitors can witness the Bay of Fundy's incredible tides - the highest in the world. Watching the ocean rise and fall dramatically within hours is an unforgettable experience for both kids and adults.

Family Travel Tips -

- **Timing is everything:** Spring and summer bring lush greenery and open attractions, while fall offers dazzling foliage and quieter roads.
- **Pack for variety:** Even short day trips can involve coastal breezes, shaded trails, and rural roads - *layers and sturdy footwear are always smart.*
- **Mix active and restful stops:** Alternate between hiking or exploring and relaxing at a café, beach, or picnic area to keep everyone energized.
- **Bring local snacks:** Farmers' markets and roadside stands are part of the experience - *grab blueberry jam, local cider, or fresh bread for a picnic treat.*
- **Leave space for surprises:** Many small communities host impromptu events - *from craft fairs to lobster suppers* - that are worth detouring for.

Fun Facts -

- The **Musquodoboit Trailway** follows an old railway line that once carried timber and agricultural goods - *it's now part of the **Trans Canada Trail** network.*
- The **Bedford Basin** served as a naval assembly point during both World Wars, helping coordinate Atlantic convoys.
- **Cole Harbor** was once home to NHL legend Sidney Crosby, whose roots remain a point of local pride.
- The **Bay of Fundy tides** can reach heights of over 16 meters - *higher than a five-storey building.*

Linking the Past and Present

The communities surrounding Halifax have always been more than satellites to the city, they are the threads that weave together Nova Scotia's economic and cultural fabric. From the forests of Hammonds Plains that supplied lumber for Halifax's shipyards to the fertile lands of the Annapolis Valley that fed its early settlers, these regions formed the backbone of a growing province.

In the 19th century, railways and trade routes linked the capital with its outlying districts, creating a network of industry and exchange. Bedford's shipyards, Dartmouth's mills, and Musquodoboit's farmlands all played vital roles in supporting Halifax's rise as a maritime hub. Even the smaller fishing communities, like those along the Eastern Shore, helped define the province's enduring connection to the sea.

Today, these surrounding regions continue to evolve - blending heritage with innovation. Lunenburg's boatbuilders now share space with artists and entrepreneurs; Wolfville's farms coexist with cutting-edge wineries and sustainable food ventures. Yet through it all, the sense of local pride and community resilience remains constant.

Exploring beyond Halifax offers more than just scenic views - it's a glimpse into how the province grew, how its people adapted, and how its traditions continue to thrive. Every family outing becomes a small step through living history, where past and present meet on forest trails, farm roads, and coastal highways.

So, pack your day bag, fill your thermos, and set out beyond the city. Whether you're feeding goats in Cole Harbor, pedaling along the Musquodoboit Trail, or tasting apples in the

Valley, you'll be sharing in the same simple pleasures that have connected Nova Scotians for generations.

Conclusion – Halifax, the Heart of the East Coast

Standing on the edge of Halifax Harbor, watching the sunlight dance across the rippling water, it's easy to see why this city captures hearts so effortlessly. Halifax is more than a destination on a map - it's a rhythm, a way of life, and a story that has been unfolding for nearly three centuries. Every cobblestone, every salty breeze, and every cheerful voice along the waterfront is part of the living character of Atlantic Canada's most vibrant city.

CONCLUSION – HALIFAX, THE HEART OF THE EAST COAST

A City Shaped by Sea and Spirit

Halifax has always drawn its strength from the sea. The harbor that once launched fleets and welcomed explorers now hums with ferries, sailboats, and the laughter of families strolling along the boardwalk. The ocean is Halifax's heartbeat - *it defines the weather, influences the cuisine, and inspires the people who call this place home.*

The beauty of Halifax lies in its dual nature: steeped in history, yet alive with modern energy. Walk a few blocks in any direction, and you'll pass centuries-old churches beside craft breweries, heritage homes beside art galleries. There's a balance here - a sense that progress and preservation can coexist. The result is a city that has evolved gracefully without ever losing its identity.

The Halifax Citadel still stands watch over the downtown core, its stone ramparts a reminder of a time when the city's safety depended on its walls and cannons. Today, those same ramparts offer one of the best panoramic views in the Maritimes. Below, life moves at a relaxed but confident pace - children playing in the Public Gardens, couples sharing seafood by the harbor, and students from across the world gathering at the Central Library's rooftop terrace to watch the sunset. Halifax's soul has shifted from defense to connection, from fortress to family destination.

The Family Legacy of Exploration

For traveling families, Halifax is a natural classroom and playground combined. Every corner of the city offers a chance to learn - not through textbooks, but through experiences. A visit to the Maritime Museum of the Atlantic introduces children to real shipwreck artifacts, including relics from the Titanic and stories of bravery at sea. Down the boardwalk, the Harbor Hopper's amphibious tours mix laughter with lessons in maritime history, proving that education and fun can coexist in the most memorable ways.

Across the harbor, the Dartmouth ferry continues a tradition over two centuries old - offering families not just transport, but a few unforgettable minutes of skyline views and sea spray. Parks like Point Pleasant and the Halifax Common transform afternoons into adventures, where picnics, playgrounds, and performances bring people together.

In Halifax, family travel isn't about rushing from attraction to attraction. It's about moments - feeding ducks at Sullivan's Pond, biking the Shubie Trail, or savoring a shared ice cream from a local dairy bar after a long day of sightseeing. These small, simple pleasures are what anchor family memories. They remind visitors that the heart of Halifax isn't just in its history or architecture, but in the connections forged between people - *locals and travelers alike.*

Learning, Laughter, and Discovery

Halifax's charm extends well beyond its scenic beauty. It's in the laughter echoing down Spring Garden Road after a summer street performance, in the clinking of glasses at a waterfront café, in the sight of sailboats dotting the horizon as gulls swoop overhead.

Every experience in Halifax is layered. A family visit to Citadel Hill becomes a lesson in resilience. A stop at the Seaport Farmers' Market reveals the region's agricultural bounty and cultural diversity. An afternoon in the Art Gallery of Nova Scotia sparks curiosity about

CONCLUSION – HALIFAX, THE HEART OF THE EAST COAST

local creativity - *from folk artists to celebrated painters like Maud Lewis.*

The city's festivals, too, add to its spirit of discovery. From the Halifax Jazz Festival's easy rhythms to the lively energy of the Busker Festival, families can immerse themselves in art, music, and laughter. Even during the quiet months of winter, when snow dusts the harbor and lights glow from shop windows, Halifax feels alive with warmth and welcome.

This openness is what sets Halifax apart. Visitors often comment not only on what they've seen, but on how they've *felt*. There's a friendliness here that goes beyond hospitality - *it's a genuine willingness to share stories, traditions, and smiles.* Whether you're talking with a fisherman in Eastern Passage, a student barista near the university district, or an artist at a weekend market, you'll find that Halifax's greatest gift is its people.

Encouragement for Slow, Mindful Travel

In a world that moves quickly, Halifax invites travelers to slow down. It's a city best experienced at walking pace - *one boardwalk, one café, one conversation at a time.* The rhythm of the harbor seems to ask visitors to linger: to stop and watch the ferries glide by, to listen to street musicians play folk songs, to taste fresh seafood caught just that morning.

Mindful travel in Halifax means being present - noticing the way the fog rolls in over the water, how locals greet one another by name, how the scent of the ocean drifts through the air after a rain. It means exploring not only the big attractions, but also the small, authentic moments: chatting with a local shop owner, visiting a neighborhood bakery, or hiking a trail just outside the city limits where the only sounds are wind and waves.

For families, mindful travel also means giving children the space to wonder. Halifax offers countless opportunities for exploration that encourage curiosity without the rush - watching tall ships dock at Queen's Marque, spotting seals off the coast near Peggy's Cove, or learning how tides shape the Bay of Fundy's unique ecosystem just a short drive away.

As you explore Halifax and its surroundings, take time to connect not just with the scenery, but with the stories, the layers of past and present that make Nova Scotia so compelling. Each community, from Bedford to Wolfville, adds another chapter to this living narrative.

From Fortress to Family Destination

When Halifax was founded in 1749, it was envisioned as a strategic stronghold - a bastion of British naval power guarding the North Atlantic. Soldiers built fortifications on high ground, settlers carved streets into rocky terrain, and the harbor became a center of military logistics and trade. For much of its early history, Halifax's growth was shaped by defense and duty.

Yet even in those early days, the seeds of community were being planted. Markets formed along the waterfront. Churches and schools followed. Families arrived from across Europe and North America, bringing with them traditions that would blend into the city's character. Over centuries, Halifax's identity expanded beyond the barracks and shipyards. The very forces that once made it a fortress - ***its strategic location, its people's resilience, and its access to the sea*** - would later make it a beacon of culture, commerce, and creativity.

The transformation was gradual but profound. After the Halifax

CONCLUSION – HALIFAX, THE HEART OF THE EAST COAST

Explosion of 1917 devastated much of the city, Haligonians rebuilt not only the buildings but their spirit. The tragedy became a catalyst for unity and progress, inspiring advances in urban planning, healthcare, and community care. By the late 20th century, Halifax had evolved into a hub of education, innovation, and tourism - *a city proud of its past but forward-looking in its outlook.*

Today, visitors can still trace that history through the landscape. The Citadel's cannons stand silent, overlooking modern high-rises and bustling streets. The harbor that once sheltered fleets now welcomes cruise ships and families on evening strolls. The echoes of the past blend seamlessly with the laughter of the present - *proof that Halifax's story continues to unfold, shaped by each new generation that walks its shores.*

A Lasting Impression

Every journey has a moment - **that quiet pause before departure** - when the traveler realizes they've left a piece of themselves behind. In Halifax, that moment comes easily. Maybe it's during a final walk along the waterfront, the salty wind tugging at your jacket as gulls wheel overhead. Or perhaps it's the memory of a child's laughter echoing across the Common, or the warmth of a conversation shared over chowder in a harborfront café.

To experience Halifax is to be welcomed into its rhythm - to feel the heartbeat of Nova Scotia through its people, its music, and its maritime soul. This is a city that doesn't simply show you its attractions; it shares its life with you.

For families, Halifax offers something truly rare: a destination that entertains, educates, and connects all at once. It's a place where children learn history by touching it, where parents rediscover the joy of exploration, and where every sunset over the water seems to promise a reason to return.

Looking Ahead – The Spirit Endures

As Halifax continues to grow and evolve, it remains grounded in the values that have always defined it - *resilience, community, and a deep respect for the sea*. New developments rise beside historic wharves, yet the city's heart beats in the same rhythm it always has. Sustainability, local enterprise, and cultural celebration now guide Halifax's future, ensuring that the charm travelers love today will endure for generations to come.

Halifax's story is far from over, and that's part of its allure. Each visitor adds a new layer, each family a new chapter. Whether it's your first visit or your fifth, the city finds ways to feel both familiar and new.

So linger a little longer. Wander the boardwalk one last time. Let the wind off the Atlantic remind you that this is more than just another stop along your travels, it's the heart of Canada's East Coast, a place where land, sea, and soul meet.

Because here, in Halifax, history lives not in museums alone, but in every friendly smile, every ocean breeze, and every story shared along the shore.

From fortress walls to family picnics, Halifax's journey mirrors the evolution of Nova Scotia itself - steadfast, welcoming, and ever tied to the sea. Once a defensive outpost, it has grown into a symbol of togetherness, creativity, and exploration. Its

CONCLUSION – HALIFAX, THE HEART OF THE EAST COAST

enduring
heart beats with the tides - forever changing, forever home.

Also by Brian Armstrong

Brian Armstrong's books explore the history, culture, and natural beauty of North America's most captivating destinations. Written in a warm, family-oriented style, his work blends local insight with engaging storytelling, offering readers an inviting way to experience the landmarks, traditions, and hidden gems that define each place.

Exploring Nova Scotia: A Journey Through History and Must-See Destinations
Discover the spirit of Nova Scotia through its storied past and breathtaking beauty. *Exploring Nova Scotia* guides readers from historic harbors and seaside villages to vibrant cultural hubs and natural wonders. Blending history, travel, and local insight, this book captures the province's enduring charm and invites families and travelers alike to experience its warm, maritime heart.
amazon.com/dp/B0DHCMSWJ8

Cape Breton Uncovered: A Local Guide to the Top Destinations on Canada's Most Scenic Island

From rugged coastlines to highland trails and Celtic heritage, *Cape Breton Uncovered* reveals the island's most unforgettable destinations through a local's eyes. This engaging guide highlights must-see attractions, hidden gems, and cultural treasures while celebrating the island's warm spirit, storytelling traditions, and breathtaking scenery - the perfect companion for travelers seeking authentic East Coast adventure.

amazon.com/dp/B0FHF6MPCZ

Printed in Dunstable, United Kingdom